Transcendental Meditation, also called the Science of Creative Intelligence, claims to be "a scientific technique for health and education." TM is offered to high school and college students throughout the United States by the Students' International Meditation Society, reported to be the fastest growing student movement in America.

What is SCI/TM?   Is it a religion?   A science? A philosophy?   A technique?   Or what?

...and what is behind this massive worldwide movement? Is it merely a preoccupation with Eastern mysticism?   Is it more than just a passing fad?

Is SCI/TM compatible with biblical Christianity? Should Christians practice transcendental meditation?

You will find whatever you want to know about TM in this scholarly, throughly documented study of a current phenomenon by Dr. Gordon R. Lewis.

Transcendental Meditation
   Is a term you daily see.
And, in your cogitation,
   Often ask, "Is it for me?"
For it's TM in the AM
   To begin a TM day.
Then more TM in the PM
   Just to end a TM day.
To TM or not to TM?
   That's the question, you'll agree.
Your answer's here within this book
   As plain as it can be.
So read, then pause to meditate
   (For you want more than *a* way.)
Upon this transcendental thought:
   He is Truth, Life and *The* Way.

What Everyone Should Know About
Transcendental
Meditation

Gordon R. Lewis

A Division of G/L Publications
Glendale, California, U.S.A.

To my wife
Doris,
a joyful example of
biblically directed
devotion to God
and family.

Except where otherwise noted, the Scripture quotations
in this publication are from the Revised Standard Version
of the Bible, copyrighted 1946 and 1952 by the Division
of Christian Education of the NCCC in the U.S.A., and
used by permission.

Grateful acknowledgement is made for several quotations
for *Transcendental Meditation* by Maharishi Mahesh Yogi.
© 1963 by Allied Publishers Private, Ltd.

Reprinted by arrangements with The New American Library,
Inc., New York, N.Y.

WHAT EVERYONE SHOULD KNOW ABOUT TRANSCENDENTAL
MEDITATION

A REGAL BOOK
Published by Pillar Books for Regal Books Division, G/L
Publications

Regal Books edition published January 1977

ISBN: 8307-0469-8

Library of Congress Catalog Card Number: 74-32326

Regal Books Division, G/L Publications
Glendale, California 91209
U.S.A.

Contents

1

What Is Transcendental Meditation?

The Promise

"Serenity without drugs!"

So reads the blurb on the cover of Maharishi Mahesh Yogi's major book, *Transcendental Meditation*—a glowing promise of natural tranquillity.

"Life need not be the painful struggle it is commonly represented to be. We are meant to be happy, and here is a way for everybody; a way which involves no austere discipline, no break with normal life and tradition, and which gives fuller and deeper meaning to all religions."[1]

The Source

Although the claim is frequently made that Transcendental Meditation or TM is not religious, the opening page of the Maharishi's book acknowledges its Hindu source:

"This unique book combines the practical wisdom found in the Vedic Rishis of ancient India and the scientific thinking of the present-day Western world. Maharishi's methods . . . include a series of physical and spiritual exercises which anyone can learn, and which can lead to a dynamic regeneration of the self."[2]

The Leader

The leader of Transcendental Meditation is Maharishi Mahesh Yogi. "Maha" means great, and "rishi" means sage, seer or saint. "Mahesh" is the family name. "Yogi" means a master of yoga. And "yoga" is the Hindu system of physical and mental control to obtain a state of well-being through union with the Absolute.

The Maharishi was for thirteen years the close and favored devotee of His Divinity Swami (Master) Brahmanand Saraswati Maharij (1869-1953). In 1958, as a result of the encouragement of his late teacher, Maharishi dedicated his life to the spiritual regeneration of the world. It was his stated objective to "rechannel the course of humanity."[3]

That same year, the Maharishi left his Himalayan retreat and began a tour of the West. Earlier swamis like Vivekananda and Yogananda had been invited by liberal Christians to make such tours. But Maharishi came on his own to reach the West.

The Followers

By acquiring a celebrated following, the Maharishi quickly attained fame himself. Among his most publicized devotees for a time were the singing group, the Beatles. And the movie star, Mia Farrow, also tried meditation. One of the most well-known meditators today is the New York Jets quarterback, Joe Namath, along with three other members of his team.

Less spectacularly, but probably more effectively, the Maharishi announced the end of his public activity in 1968 and then began training instructors. He has personally trained 4,400 instructors and now claims a half million meditators worldwide. In the United States alone, there are some 205 TM centers.[4]

The Program

The program for obtaining, initiating and training meditators is effectively planned. After two free introductory lectures open to the public, those who wish to learn the technique for "realizing their full mental potential and attaining a deep sense of rest" must make a commitment. They agree to take time twice a day for meditation—twenty minutes before breakfast and before dinner, pay tuition—$55 for high school students, $65 for college students, and $125 for working adults—and be off drugs for fifteen days.

Then having met these conditions, the new recruits, like Hindus, bring to the initiation session offerings of fresh flowers, fresh fruit and a clean white handkerchief. After presenting these offerings in a brief, traditional ceremony, they then hear the names of Hindu teachers who preserved the TM approach through the centuries.

At this time, the initiates are given their secret *mantra*. The mantra is a sound without meaning, but with known effects.[5]

Then for each of three successive days, the initiate receives two hours of personal instruction. During the next month he attends follow-up sessions once a week. Checkers ask questions of him to determine how well his meditation is progressing.

Throughout the first year, there is a "tune-up" session once a month for the meditator. Those with special interests in TM may take advanced courses in subsequent years.[6]

The Movement

The extensive training of TM has produced several organized wings of the movement. The Spiritual Regeneration Movement (SRM) was founded by the Maharishi in England for adults interested in philosophical and spiritual values. For high school and college students in the United States, he established the Students' International Meditation Society (SIMS). Called the fastest growing student movement in the United States, centers of SIMS are in over 1,000 colleges in the U.S.A. The International Meditation Society (IMS) offers courses to the general public.

The present name under which the TM viewpoint and discipline is presented is the Science of Creative Intelligence (SCI). The American Foundation for the Science of Creative Intelligence (AFSCI) offers courses to business and industry. Throughout the presentations of TM/SCI, teachers scrupulously avoid all religious terminology. Courses in SCI cover the doctrinal or "scientific" aspects of the yoga system, while TM courses offer practical methods of meditation. Classes in both SCI and TM have been legalized for the use in the public schools of Illinois and are offered for credit in the public schools of New York, Massachusetts, Florida and California.[7]

In 1971, the Maharishi International University (MIU) opened in Los Angeles. Now MIU's central campus occupies the 232-acre site of the former Parsons College at Fairfield, Iowa. It plans to develop 3,600 centers for the training of SCI teachers—one center per million population throughout the world.

Each center, in turn, seeks to train 1,000 teachers by means of a 33-lecture video course prepared especially for this purpose by the Maharishi.

The Claims

As to what TM is or is not, the more recent central claims it makes for itself are contrary to earlier religious expressions of TM's significance. When I attended the introductory lectures at the Denver Center for the Science of Creative Intelligence in the spring of 1974, the chairman first emphasized what TM is not:

TM is not a philosophy. It is not a life-style requiring a diet of curry or the practice of difficult exercises. It is not a trance; the mediator is aware of his environment even though he does not respond to it. TM is not a religion. It is, however, religiously significant, compatible with Christianity and other faiths.

What then is TM and what does it do for a person?

TM is allegedly a scientific technique enabling one "to do less and accomplish more." It supposedly allows a person to use his full mental potential and yet attain a deep sense of rest. These attractive goals are said to be realized by leading the awareness inward rather than outward. Consequently, the mind is attracted from the gross levels of thought to increasingly subtle thoughts until it arrives at its Source—Pure Creative Intelligence.[8]

The Meditators

What do meditators say they have received from TM? TM, we are told, has been effective in relieving stress and freeing people from addiction to drugs, alcohol and tobacco.

"I'm more relaxed now," says Eddie Bell, a New York Jets football player. "The first time I really did it I was amazed at the effect. After twenty minutes of it, I felt refreshed, like I'd slept seven or eight hours. I felt like I had my whole day ahead of me. It was like I'd been in a much deeper form of relaxation."[9]

A California assemblyman, Ken Meade, said, "It gave me clarity of thought to make decisions, such as not to leave public office. It released anxiety and tension and things that were impending my ability to function. It enabled me to get some rest after six weeks of no sleep."[10]

And California state Senator Arlen Gregorio says, "TM changed my life. I'm more stable emotionally. I don't get depression after high-pitched tension. I think I'm able to be more effective."[11]

The Confirmation?

The case for the effectiveness of TM in producing a state of "restful alertness" is not solely dependent upon anecdotes of famous people. Appeal is made to scientific research in several different areas: breath rate, cardiac output, biochemical changes, brain wave patterns, reaction time, perceptual ability, motor performance, learning ability, etc. In each of these areas, R.K. Wallace, president of MIU, claims objective demonstration for positive effects from regular practice of TM.[12]

We cannot here evaluate the tests alleged to demonstrate TM's value psychologically and physically. This has been attempted already in a three-part article by Colin Campbell, Gary E. Schwartz and Leon S. Otis in *Psychology Today,* early in 1974.

Leon Otis of Stanford University's Research Institute's staff found:

11

"TM has little effect on heart rate or blood pressure, and that the simple act of resting every day over a three-month period may produce more alpha waves than meditation."[13]

A comparison of self-images of meditators and a control group did not differ significantly, leading to Otis' conclusion, "I don't believe, therefore, that TM alters basic personality."[14]

Gary Schwartz explains that the TM studies "left open the question of whether other forms of meditation might yield comparable results."[15]

Schwartz then adds, "The significance of changes in skin resistance remains somewhat obscure . . . . The obscurity is compounded by the imprecision of words like 'relaxed,' 'alert' and 'aroused.' "[16]

With respect to the use of drugs, Schwartz says, "The assertion, in short, that TM cures drug abuse may be true but remains unproven."[17]

Schwartz further states, "Probably the most controversial claim made for TM is that it increases 'creative intelligence.' " In this respect, he wisely questions the ideal of restful alertness through TM: "It is worth asking, though, if relaxation is the right state for *all* kinds of activities. Basic research indicates that too much or too little arousal can lead to inferior performance."[18]

At the present stage of investigation, Schwartz's conclusion is justified:

"There are still a good many mysteries about meditation, and there are several versions of how it works. For this reason I think we should remain wary of the claims and selective use of scientific data by well-meaning but scientifically unsophisticated practitioners."[19]

12

Expressing reservations similar to those of Schwartz, Harrison Pope, Jr., a meditator and medical student, says, "I do feel that TM has more than once endangered its reputation among educated people by prematurely broadcasting scientific findings of tentative caliber."[20]

At the same time, many of the phenomena produced by TM are also produced by a scientific technique called biofeedback, quite apart from Hindu presuppositions about Being, consciousness and bliss. According to biofeedback specialist Barbara Brown:

"Both meditation and alpha training can produce the sensation of separation from the material universe, a depersonalization, loss of individual identity, and an awareness of the unifying thread of life."[21]

The Issue

The question still remains: whether TM is simply a scientific matter of voluntary control of internal functions like biofeedback, or a religiously motivated and interpreted control of internal functions, as Colin Campbell concluded, "clearly a revival of ancient Indian Brahmanism and Hinduism."[22]

TM has moved into the public school system on the negative claim that it is a purely scientific technique and not a religion or a philosophy. The case for TM in public schools rests on this claim.

TM has attracted people in the churches by claiming that the benefits of TM can be experienced without giving up Christianity. The appeal to Christians is based on the affirmative claim that TM is taught by Jesus Christ and the writers of the Bible.[23] The case for TM in Christendom rests on this claim.

It is of great importance, therefore, to educators and collegians, parents and children, pastors and

13

church members to determine whether TM is in fact a religion—a form of Hinduism.

Footnotes

1. Maharishi Mahesh Yogi, *Transcendental Meditation* (Original title: *The Science of Being and Art of Living*) (New York: New American Library, 1968), frontis page.
2. *Ibid.*
3. Charles F. Lutes, "Preface," Maharishi Mahesh Yogi, *Trascendental Meditation: The Science of Being and Art of Living* (Bergenfield, New Jersey: New American Library, 1963), pp. xii, xiii.
4. Jerry Daniels, Introductory Lecture, March 6, 1974, Denver Center for the Science of Creative Intelligence.
5. *Ibid.*
6. *Ibid.*
7. David Haddon, "New Plant Thrives in a Spiritual Desert," *Christianity Today* (December 21, 1973), pp. 9-12.
8. Jerry Daniels, *op. cit.*
9. A TM reprint, "These Four Jets Are Meditating" from the *New York Post* (September 20, 1973).
10. A TM reprint, "Meditation Irons Furrowed Brows in State Legislative Halls" from the *San Francisco Examiner* (Sunday, June 10, 1973).
11. *Ibid.*
12. R. K. Wallace, *Scientific Research on Transcendental Meditation* (Los Angeles: MIU, 1972), pamphlet.
13. Leon A. Otis, "The facts on Transcendental Meditation: Part III," *Psychology Today* (April, 1974), p. 46.
14. *Ibid.*
15. Gary E. Schwartz, "The Facts on Transcendental Meditation: Part II," *Psychology Today* (April, 1974), pp. 39-44.
16. *Ibid.*
17. *Ibid.*
18. *Ibid.*
19. *Ibid.*
20. Harrison Pope, Jr., *The Road East: America's New Discovery of Eastern Wisdom* (Boston: Beacon Press, 1974), p. 37.
21. Barbara B. Brown, *New Mind, New Body: Biofeedback: New Directions for the Mind* (New York: Harper & Row, 1974), condensed in *Psychology Today* (August, 1974), p. 106.
22. Colin Campbell, "The Facts on Transcendental Meditation: Part I," *Psychology Today* (April, 1974), p. 38.
23. Maharishi, *Transcendental Meditation*, pp. 253,254.

2

What Is the Source of Man and His Existence?

Some meditators I talked with in Colorado Springs once told me, "We just practice the TM technique for its benefits. We don't want to think about its meaning."

They were like people high on drugs who prefer not to consider exactly what they are taking! Meditators and prospective meditators owe it to themselves to understand as much as possible about their technique and its outcome.

Understanding has not prevented Maharishi Mahesh Yogi from enjoying the benefits of the technique. And he considers understanding so important that he devoted the first major section of his book, *Transcendental Meditation,* to "the science of Being" before discussing "the art of living."

But to understand SCI/TM, it is necessary first to understand what the Maharishi means by the creative intelligence which is the source of every thought and perception. So let's begin with a look at the teachings of the Maharishi, and then take a look at the relationship of his teachings to both the Hindu and Christian views of (1) man's Source; and (2) man's relation to his Source.

The Hindu View: Man's Source

In each meditation session, restful alertness comes through a direct consciousness of man's Source. "The technique may be defined," the Maharishi writes, "as turning the attention inwards toward subtler levels of thought until the mind transcends the experience of the subtlest state of the thought and arrives at the source of thought."[1]

The objective of TM, in the Maharishi's words, is direct experience of pure Being. In order to grasp this very basic point, we need to remember that "most Indian thinkers are apt to emphasize universal concepts and to subordinate the concrete individual and the particular perception to the universal."[2]

Hajime Nakamura goes on to illustrate this very point in his *Ways of Thinking of Eastern Peoples*. Instead of saying, "He becomes old," the Sanskrit says, "He goes to oldness." Putting ourselves in this way of thinking we might say, the more important thing is not your particular car, but "carness"; not your dog, but "dogness"; not yourself as distinct from all others, but your humanness—which you share with all other persons. And even more important is what carness, dogness and humanness share in common: existence, Being.

Like many other Indian thinkers, Maharishi gives prominence to universal existence as distinct from the particular things that exist in the observable world. He writes, "We may say that existence is the life itself while that which exists is the ever-changing phenomenal phase (cars, dogs, people) of the never-changing reality of existence—Being."[3,4]

He then adds, "Existence is the abstract aspect of life on which are built what we call the concrete

Reality of everything that is. Since this... everything in... Absolute alone is real, everything... Absolute. The... nothing but manifest Absolute. The... ated, therefore, but emanates f... eternally. Consequently, all... persons and things are re... biography and history... appearance only.

The Hindu
Source
Insc...
stra...

"...changing Unity of life which underlies the evident multiplicity of creation, for Reality is both manifest and unmanifest, and That alone is. 'I am That, thou are That and all this is That,' is the Truth; and this is the kernel of the Vedic teaching, which the rishis extol as teaching 'worthy of hearing, contemplating and realizing.' "[8]

As in Hinduism, since Being is one, TM finds that the idea of many beings is illusory or "maya." Maharishi explains, "The word 'maya' means literally that which is not, that which does not exist . . . it is not anything substantial."[9]

Maya relates the absolute—Brahman—to the relative aspect of life as the sap relates to the tree. "Every fibre of the tree is nothing but the sap. Sap, while remaining sap, appears as the tree. Likewise, through the influence of maya, Brahman, remaining Brahman appears as the manifested world."[10]

The impersonal Absolute is the one, unchanging

unchanging
the cosmos is
world is not cre-
om the divine Being
the changing particular
ative and illusory. So your
in general are in the realm of

iew: Man's Relation to His

ar as things, animals and people share ab-
ct Existence, they are emanations of the divine
Being and themselves divine. Consequently, "every
object, no matter how humble, contains within itself
all degrees of manifestation, from the 'grossest'
(most material) to the very subtlest *and beyond*—to
the unmanifest Absolute itself."[11]

Insofar as things, animals and people are distinct
from each other and begin, change and pass away,
they are illusory. Therefore, the realm of diversity of
which we are ordinarily conscious is actually only an
unreal "appearance."

The Maharishi sees the "evolution of the universe
as a cyclical process, with a beginning and an end;
moreover, the cycle is believed to repeat itself indefi-
nitely . . . . According to this concept the Absolute is manifesting continuously and dynamically so
that there is a continuous outflow of the energy
which is the power that keeps everything going."[12]

Such a concept, however, reduces history, with its
unique persons and events to an endless, meaningless
series of cycles. Consequently, a person's biography
is a pointless part of the futile cycle of concrete par-
ticulars.

"The present phenomenal phase of existence is seen to have no permanent significance."[13] (The realization of this teaching in TM that one's life is lacking in significance may lead a meditator not only to relaxation, but also to fatalistic apathy!)

Although God is not the changing world of ordinary knowledge and experience, the Source of all this is not supernatural. God is not the Lord of life and nature in a transcendent sense. Because the Maharishi's god—Brahman—is not personal or transcendent to the universe, it can never perform miracles to redeem people unable to save themselves.

When claiming that one reaches a state of pure awareness, TM means that one comes in contact with the Absolute. But in contacting one's Source, transcendental meditator Anthony Campbell says:

"No supernatural agency is being invoked. The world remains subject to natural law . . . . Events occurring in the space-time world are explicable without exception by natural causes. (Maharishi has said that miracles are natural events whose causes we do not understand.) The concept of the Absolute is in no sense inconsistent with the naturalistic principle."[14]

The Christian View: Man's Source

Christian thought about the world's Source agrees that material things owe their existence to God (Gen. 1:1). God made the world and is active in every part of nature (Ps. 104:1-35). Yet, though the God of Christianity is active in the world He made, He is distinct from it (1 Kings 8:27).

Reality is not a one-story, ranch-house type of reality; it has two stories. The upper story includes the triune God alone, and the lower story includes

19

created angels, men, animals, vegetation and nature.

Because God ordinarily works in uniform ways through nature, its laws are uniform. But the God of the Bible is Absolute in the sense of being independent of all creation, unlimited by space and time and self-determined—sovereign and free. So God can act independently of nature, performing miracles in history according to His purpose of grace (Heb. 2:4).[15]

Because God is over nature, He can and does for His redemptive purposes, act in unusual, supernatural ways. Supernaturally God created the world, raised Christ from the dead and will bring the present age to an abrupt end at the return of Christ in power and glory.[16] Christianity allows for any truth in naturalism, but is not limited to a naturalistic, single-level view of reality.

God is never to be confused with any aspect of the temporal world. He is not the most universal characteristic of houses, cows or even man. His eternal Being transcends not only our thoughts about Him, but also the world's temporal, finite being, however abstract (Acts 17:24-29).

The creation does not manifest God's being, but is His handiwork. Christians know that all things do not eternally emanate from the divine Being, but were once-and-for-all freely and purposefully created by God out of nothing (Pss. 33:6,9; 148:5).

The "sap" of the world's trees is not divine. Finite energy or being had a beginning, whereas the divine Being is eternal (Ps. 102:26,27). The being of the world is dependent; God's Being is independent. The world is material; God is spirit, unlimited by space (John 4:24; Luke 24:39).

Alan Watts, popular interpreter of Indian thought, sees clearly the incompatibility of Hindu and Christian views of creation. In the world view of the Hindus, the cosmos is the "hide-and-seek game"—*lila*—of the Self (Absolute common to us all). But in the Christian and theistic world view—shared to some extent by Jews and Muslims, all things are created by the will of God out of nothing.

Created objects—be they animal, vegetable or mineral—are "not parts or aspects or manifestations of God, not roles that he is playing. For between the Creator and the creature there is an infinite difference . . . because the creature is fundamentally and absolutely other than the Creator, the creature is always in peril of the final and irremeable disaster of going off on its own way so far as to lose fellowship with its Creator forever."[17]

Alan Watts opts for Hinduism, but admits, "If the Christian view of the world is true, the Hindu cannot be true."[18]

The Christian View:
Man's Relation to His Source

God is not unmanifested; He disclosed Himself in His Son Jesus Christ and through His specially chosen and prepared prophets and apostles (Heb. 1:1; 2 Pet. 1:19-21; Eph. 3:5).

Yet man himself is not a manifestation of divine Being; he is the product of divine creativity. In soul and body, man is created by God—not begotten by God. A manufacturer makes a car; he begets a son.

Only Christ is uniquely begotten of God the Father and so of the same divine nature (John 1:1,14-18); human beings in general are made by God in God's image and likeness (Gen. 1:27). Christ is eternally of the divine Being (John 17:5); man was

21

created in time by God, not out of the divine Being, but his body out of dust (Gen. 2:7).

So although man is not simply made by God like things, but is made in the image of God, he is made. He has not emanated from God's being. As created, man is different from God; as a being made in the divine likeness, man has some characteristics analogous to God's. But man's being is not divine Being.

Man's soul was created out of nothing and faces an endless eternal existence in the future, but was not eternally existent in the past. Man's mind and sense are real and, as created in the divine likeness, have a value and dignity that should not be "removed" or denigrated (Prov. 20:12; Rom. 12:1,2). Each human life in this temporal scene is of eternal value and significance in carrying out God's eternal purpose in history (Matt. 16:26,27). History is not a cyclical process, but a linear one.

The present temporal realm of individual existence has eternal significance in God's plan. This life is not one of thousands of reincarnations, but a unique, once-for-all opportunity (Heb. 9:27) to respond to divine revelation in nature (Rom. 1:20), the human heart (Rom. 2:14,15), the Old Testament and the New Testament (2 Tim. 3:15-17). The way to help others, in turn, is to believe, teach and exemplify this revealed truth which manifests the actual will of God for men today.

So, though man is not part of the divine Being, as forgiven, renewed and glorified on the basis of Christ's atonement, he need not fear death (Heb. 2:-14,15). Rather, the Christian anticipates an eternity of joyful and meaningful fellowship with a personal triune God (John 14:1-3; 1 Thess. 4:17).

Yes, the God of the Bible is not only distinct from

the universe, but personal. God is a conscious, active Spirit. But the Creator of persons could hardly be less than personal. He knows (Matt. 6:8,32), loves (1 John 4:8-10), wills (Matt. 6:10; 12:50) and acts (Exod. 14:13,31; Luke 1:49).

It may seem that Christians limit God by referring to Him as personal. But in reference to God, "person" must be freed from ordinary human limitation of space, time and evil. For God has unlimited power to know, love and act in the fullest and best senses consistent with His holy nature.[19]

About this time, transcendental meditators tend to say, "The matter has become too intellectual. The important thing is experiencing tranquillity through meditation. All doctrinal distinctions are inadequate." The difference, however, between the TM Source and the Christian's God is not merely conceptual; it reflects a difference of experienced reality.

In practice, does one meditate upon the being of the universe or its transcendent Creator? Made to know, love and serve the living God, man is never finally fulfilled until his mind, affections and determinations are centered upon God Himself.

True teaching about God, therefore, is the key to fulfilling experience of God. Confusing God with man or nature is worship and service of the creation more than the Creator. However subtle and devout this may be, it is sin (see Rom. 1:25).

An Indian convert to Christianity vividly portrayed the practical importance of the truth that God is personal. If God were abstract Being, he explained, people would be the victims of a blind, heartless "karma"—law of justice—what you sow you reap. But we need not despair if above the inexorable law of justice we are loved by a merciful divine Person.

In our own human experience we know that a father is not unloving to his son. If his son falls into a bad habit like getting drunk, his father does not treat him on the basis of strict karma alone. Normally a father is loving and merciful to a disobedient son. A father bears the sorrow his son causes with the earnest desire to win him back to a better life.

Can God deal with us with less mercy, love and patience? If God is not merciful to us, then He is not a person. But if He is merciful, then He is a person.[20]

Because God is personal, He has a grand design of holy love for history—and for men's lives in time and space. Because God is distinct and personal, He can act supernaturally on the basis of Christ's atonement to save the lost. Because God is personal, He can welcome repentant sinners back to Himself.

Because God is personal, he can forgive sinners and declare believers as righteous as their substitute, Jesus Christ. Because God is personal, Christians can cry out to Him and know that their prayer is heard and answered.

The belief that God is personal—the tri-personal Father, Son and Holy Spirit—is no mere abstract doctrine. It is the key to fellowship with God and all the richness of Christian experience.

In summary, God is not bliss-consciousness, nor the human soul. He is not a mindless, contentless abstraction from nature or man. He is not the highest abstraction of the human mind.

But the Source the Maharishi seeks in TM is mere abstract Being. His monistic world view is plainly not "scientific," but is a version of the Hindu religion.

And the Hindu mind tends to think in universal abstractions and makes the mistake of deifying them.

The God of TM is not the God of Jesus Christ or the Bible. Even when the Maharishi speaks of God as personal, he is not referring to the transcendent miracle-working God who raised Christ from the dead. Any Christian who attempts to practice TM with any understanding of its objective becomes unfaithful to the Bible's transcendent, tri-personal Creator, Redeemer and Counselor.

Footnotes

1. Maharishi Mahesh Yogi, *On the Bhagavad-Gita: A New Translation and Commentary*, Chapters 1-6 (Baltimore: Penguin Books, 1967), p. 470.
2. Hajime Nakamura, *Ways of Thinking of Eastern Peoples: India-China-Tibet-Japan* (Honolulu: East-West Center Press, 1964), p. 45.
3. Maharishi, *Transcendental Meditation*, p. 21.
4. This concept of Being and universal existence is also called monism or monistic being.
5. Maharishi, *Transcendental Meditation*, p. 21.
6. *Ibid.*, pp. 2-22.
7. Panentheism is the doctrine that God includes the world as a part of—though not the whole of—His Being. Pantheism is the doctrine that God is the transcendent reality of which the material universe and man are only manifestations; it involves a denial of God's personality and expresses a tendency to equate God with the forces and laws of the universe.
8. Maharishi, *On the Bhagavad-Gita*, p. 9.
9. *Ibid.*, pp. 491,492.
10. *Ibid.*, pp. 491,492.
11. Anthony Campbell, *Seven States of Consciousness: A Vision of Possibilities Suggested by the Teaching of Maharishi Yogi* (New York: Harper and Row, 1974), p. 81.
12. *Ibid.*
13. Maharishi, *On the Bhagavad-Gita* (II, 28), p. 105.
14. Anthony Campbell, *op. cit.*, p. 81.
15. C.S. Lewis, *Miracles,* (New York: The Macmillan Company, 1948), p. 128. This book is recommended for discussion of the possibility of miracles.
16. On the purposes of miracles, see my *Judge for Yourself,* (Downers Grove, Illinois: Inter-Varsity Press, 1974), pp. 46-60.
17. Alan Watts, Beyond Theology: *The Art of Godmanship,* (New York: Vintage Books, 1964), pp. 197-98.
18. *Ibid.*
19. C.S. Lewis, *Mere Christianity.* (New York: The Macmillan Company, 1952), pp. 118-129.
20. G. D. Yisudas, *One God Many Manifestations,* (Bombay, India: Gospel Literature Service, 1969), pp. 7,8.

26

3

What Is Man's Basic Problem?

Now let's look at the teachings of Maharishi Mahesh Yogi and their relationship to Hidu and Christian views of (1) man's need; and (2) the prescription for meeting that need.

The Hindu View: Man's Need

According to the diagnosis of the Maharishi, man's deepest difficulty is his lack of consciousness of his own divine Being. Instead of attaining consciousness of God, people try to be good or merely think about God. "All the misery in the world is due to missing this one point."[1]

Generation after generation fails to realize contact with Being and thus resolve the opposition between the relative and the Absolute in their consciousness. "That has been the main reason for the growing suffering, misery, and tension and the increasing negativity in all fields of activity."[2]

How does one attain consciousness of unity with abstract Being? A person needs to expand his consciousness through seven distinguishable states. These have been explained by Anthony Campbell in his *Seven States of Consciousness: A Vision of Pos-*

sibilities Suggested by the Teaching of Maharishi Mahesh Yogi.[3]

According to Campbell, people need to move beyond the three ordinary states of consciousness which are: (1) consciousness of dreamless sleep; (2) consciousness of dreaming; and (3) waking awareness of the self as both mind and body, and individual.

According to TM, a person needs to be liberated from these to attain (4) a consciousness of his Self—Hindu "atman"—or soul alone. The body and everything which is not Self must cease to exist. This is called a state of transcendental consciousness because it goes beyond the relative appearances of the senses concerning the reality of the body. However, this state of consciousness does not resolve man's problems.

People also need (5) a state of cosmic consciousness. In this state one attains a greatly enhanced knowledge of reality, but one which is yet incomplete. An even more subtle level becomes necessary, (6) the state of God-consciousness.

But even this state is not a sense of fellowship with a personal Lord of the universe. As Campbell explains, "Maharishi is not talking about God as an object of belief or even primarily of worship; he is saying that to someone whose awareness has reached this state the world is "glorified" and takes on a personal quality."[4]

The God-consciousness of TM, therefore, is actually a glorified personification of the world; it is not the God-consciousness of Christians—a personal I/Thou fellowship through the witness of the Holy Spirit.

Man's ultimate need, according to TM, is for (7) a state of consciousness called Unity. In the experience of Unity a person sees both aspects of life—the ever-changing relative and the unchanging Absolute—simultaneously and as one. The Absolute-relative paradox, irresolvable to conceptual thought or words, is allegedly resolved in the perception of Unity. This, Campbell acknowledges, is the consciousness of which the Upanishads—a class of Vedic writings—speak in the statement, "All this is Brahman."[5]

The Hindu View: Meeting Man's Need

Since man's great need is to "go from the field of sensory activity to that of mental activity, until, transcending the subtlest mental activity, he approaches the field of pure Being,"[6] he needs a technique to make this possible. He needs a method to help him evolve through each of the seven stages of consciousness.

The method should help him be more relaxed, more rested, more alert, more perceptive and more stable than he has been before. It should teach him to alternate periods of rest and productivity. It should give him an inner peace that comes only through liberation from space-time limitations.

TM claims to offer the simplest, most effective method for attaining consciousness of one Unity—absorption into Brahman. Clearly then, TM is the way not simply to relaxation, but to a consciousness with respect to the nature of reality that is a form of the Hindu religion and philosophy.

So man's greatest need is to practice TM! It enables people to accept the world of diversity as an illusion of divine play and to stand inwardly apart from it. It seeks to help people pass from the personal self and be absorbed in the impersonal Essence, Brah-

29

man. And when the raindrop slips into the shining sea the problems of the self are over.

Self-realization cults always spell the Self with a capital "S," meaning you are to realize yourself as God. But this quest of self as the Self never succeeds.

A missionary to India for some fifty years said, "I have searched India from the Himalayas to Cape Cormorin for over half a century to find a person who has arrived at the realization of the self and become the Self, become God. I have never found one.

"It is an illusion. The Self is created, a creature, and can never become the Creator."[7]

The Christian View: Man's Need

Man's basic problem is his insolence against his Creator, not a lack of consciousness of his own divinity. Knowing his wise and powerful Creator's demands of righteousness, man inexcusably worships and serves the creature more than the Creator (Rom. 1:25).

According to Christianity, therefore, the basic need of men is neither self-realization nor self-mortification. Christ calls sinners to self-surrender and self-renewal. The Lord of all wants you, your self. The Lord wants not merely your time, your loyalty, your trust, your service, your money, but your self in self-surrender.

The self is not canceled when surrendered. It is heightened. It is renewed in knowledge, righteousness and true holiness (Eph. 4:24; Col. 3:10).

By the grace of God you need to become like Christ who said, "Not my will, but thine, be done" (Luke 22:42, *KJV*). "You are not a worm, nor a wonder. You are an ordinary fallen self who needs to become extraordinary."

Man's great need is to be cleansed of selfishness, sin and its subtle effects. And this is entirely possible, for by the Spirit of grace through the Word, you can become the person God created and redeemed you to be.[8]

So man's problem is not to transcend the body with its finite limitations in space and time. As created, the body—male and female—with everything else was "very good" (Gen. 1:31). God created the senses not to play tricks on us, but that we might know and rule the world (Prov. 20:12).

Man's real problem is self-centeredness. He suffers from a selfish use of his body, not from a consciousness of its individuality. Bodily activities are not inherently evil nor good, but instrumental either to good or to evil (Rom. 6:12-14; 1 Tim. 4:3-8).

So Christians do not need liberation from the body, but divine wisdom and self-control in the use of it. Our basic need is to surrender the body to the service of God (Rom. 12:1,2). The body is to be offered to God as a living sacrifice; its members serving as instruments of righteousness, not of sin.

The Christian also anticipates a resurrected body through which to praise and serve God eternally.

Self-surrender of the whole person, body and soul, is required because we have staged a revolution against the rule of God. God cannot welcome us back into His personal fellowship until we repent of making ourselves His enemies. Alienated and estranged from God, we need to be *reconciled*.

Self-surrender is necessary, furthermore, because we have become compulsive rebels against God's wise purposes of holy love. Jesus who knew the heart of men said, "I tell you the truth; everyone who sins is a slave of sin" (John 8:34, *TEV*). Unable to liber-

31

ate ourselves from the slave market of sin, we must be *redeemed*. We need Christ's redemption to set us free from our tensions, anxieties, selfishness and greed. In repentant faith, we receive the ransom He paid.

As willful sinners, we have not only violated God, ourselves and others, but divine justice. We need to be *forgiven*. Before the moral law, the inexorable law of karma, we all stand guilty. The best of us comes short and misses the mark. No one is declared righteous by observing the law. Rather, through the law we become conscious of sin (Rom. 3:9-20).

We all know that we have not always loved God with our whole being and our neighbors as ourselves (Matt. 22:37-40). When we have offended loved ones on earth over and over again, we need more than a superficial apology; we need genuine repentance. Through self-surrender we restore the necessary respect and love. So before a holy God we need to repent and believe in his purposes of grace, to be forgiven all our sin and given the perfect righteousness of our Saviour Jesus Christ.

The Christian View: Meeting Man's Need

To meditate for days and months and years to attain a state of transcendental consciousness in which everything—sensory knowledge, the body, the observable world, history, science, society, the home, political power—not the Self ceases to exist is unrealistic and idolatrous. It is not spiritual, but sinful, for it disregards and despises the world God created and sustains.

From a Christian standpoint, it is equally unrealistic to idealize a permanent state of "bliss-consciousness." The Christian recognizes man's need for an abiding joy, but has no illusions that life in a fallen world with a sinful heart can be free from all suffering. A person should not be given the unrealistic hope of attaining a state of bliss beyond all duty and responsibility.

The human predicament is such that no mere expansion of consciousness will do. We need help from beyond ourselves, help from God. We need personal fellowship with a personal Lord. His gracious activity alone can restore us to His fellowship, in His sight.

Unfortunately, this is not what TM means by God-consciousness. A personification of energy, nature or the sum total of the universe is not the transcendent Creator and Redeemer. A sinner needs acceptance with the holy One who cannot look with favor upon his sinfulness.

TM may, like aspirin, temporarily alleviate some of the symptoms of man's illness, but no amount of medication in any number of lives can reconcile sinners to a holy God, supernaturally regenerate their hearts and objectively justify them before God's moral law.

The ultimate goal of the Christian is never to be indistinguishable from the totality of reality in an undifferentiated unity. Rather, people need a fellowship with God that is eternal and unbroken; a fellowship not dependent upon their own often inadequate efforts, but upon the grace of God and the free gift of Christ's perfect righteousness.

Man's great need then is for justification—forgiveness from all his sins and the imputation to him of the righteousness of Christ. By simple faith, man needs to be born again from above and given new life by the Holy Spirit. Only then can he enter the Kingdom of God (John 3:3-7).

The method man needs is not one of persuading himself of what really is not so, but a way of hearing the gospel meaningfully, responding to it sincerely and growing in grace and knowledge of the Lord Jesus Christ. He needs a method endued with power from beyond himself, a supernatural God who can answer prayer and help in time of need.

The method man needs is one that is not wholly dependent upon his own weak or strong efforts. It must move in the direction of truth and reality, not of false idealism. For this purpose God gave the guidance of propositional truth in Scripture.

The method men need, therefore, is a biblical method. Whatever temporary benefits may be achieved by TM, there is no eternal life apart from the hearing of the gospel of the Christ who died for our sins and rose again according to the Scriptures (2 John 9).

Summing up then, in TM and Christianity we find two incompatible diagnoses of man's basic need. If men need what Christianity insists upon, TM and Hinduism are superficial and deceptive. Christians admittedly enjoy meditating upon their triune God and His marvelous plan of redemption as revealed in Scripture, but they do not imagine that by meditating they can attain perfection.

Footnotes

1. *Meditations of Maharishi Mahesh Yogi* (New York: Bantam Books, 1968), p. 60.
2. Maharishi, *Transcendental Meditation*, p. 42.
3. Anthony Campbell, *op. cit.*
4. *Ibid.*, p. 94.
5. *Ibid.*, p. 98.
6. Maharishi, *On the Bhagavad-Gita*, p. 480.
7. E. Stanley Jones, *Victory Through Surrender* (Nashville: Abingdon Press, 1966), p. 27.
8. *Ibid.*, pp. 28-46.

4

What Has the Spiritual Leader Done to Meet Man's Need?

We are now ready to look at the teachings of Maharishi Mahesh Yogi and their relationship to Hindu and Christian views of what the spiritual leader has done to meet man's need.

The Hindu View:
What the Spiritual Leader Has Done

The founder and leader of Transcendental Meditation is a yogi. But what does the title of "Yogi" mean? A yogi, the Maharishi Mahesh explains, is a person who has striven for righteousness for countless years in previous existences. And now in this reincarnation, according to the law of karma, he is finally born into one of the few families of yogis.[1]

As a result of this evolvement, he has a chance very early in this life of realizing God-consciousness. Quickly he learns to control the senses, thoughts and breath so that he lives in the world he can be unattached. Things and evil fall off him like water off a lotus leaf—hence, the references to the lotus feet of the gurus.

As a yogi, he comes to see that the being of an evolved man and that of animals—cow, elephant or dog—is the same. The highest yogi sees everything, even pleasure and pain, with an even vision,[2] and, in this sense, is said to have attained evenness of vision.[3]

But a yogi strives for even greater perfection. With a zeal developed over the ages and perfected through his many births, he strives to move on through the seven stages of consciousness to reach his goal. As an individual distinct from Being, he ceases to exist. He becomes pure Existence.[4]

As one of the very few who have attained, Maharishi Mahesh seeks to exemplify for others the evenness of vision that is possible and to show them how they, too, can strive for Unity or pure Existence. As an example and as a teacher, he has sought to spread these teachings throughout the world and to establish the method of TM in the accomplishment of his goals.

The Maharishi does not claim to have originated his technique. It came to him through a long line of Indian and Hindu sages—holy masters—which are named at the TM initiation ceremony,[5] and from the *Bhagavad-Gita*.

The Maharishi claims only to be a transmitter of ancient human wisdom and a manifestation of abstract Being. He claims no supernatural birth, character, miracles, teaching or authority. But since all man needs is an expanded consciousness, his teaching and personal example are sufficient.

The Christian View:
What the Spiritual Leader Has Done

Given the previous diagnosis of man's predicament, it is clear that the best teaching and a model are not enough. These cannot remove the just verdict of condemnation, nor regenerate the human heart, nor reconcile estranged man to God.

Man cannot do any of these things for himself. Only God can provide them. And God the Father has done so in God the Son, the Substitute who did for man what he could not do for himself. God disclosed this remarkable plan of salvation through supernaturally inspired prophets in the holy Scriptures.

Hence, Christians realize that man's hope lies in a Person—not in a mere technique—a person who does not originate from beneath like the rest of fallen man, but from above—from God (John 8:32).

The first sign of the appearance of the God-man on earth was Jesus' virgin birth (Matt. 1:23). Jesus Christ is not the end result of centuries of human transmigration and self-effort. Eternally in fellowship with God the Father as the second person of the Trinity, Jesus Christ was the unique once-for-all incarnation of God (Acts 4:12). And His person was never reduced to the mere abstraction of "Existence." He is a living, loving, all-powerful Saviour and Lord.

Jesus is not merely a transmitter of human wisdom attained from nature and passed on by sages. More than that, He is a communicator of special revelation given directly from God and shared with us through inspired apostles. Having come from the transcendent, supernatural realm, Christ brought divine revelation (Heb. 1:1-3). Throughout His earthly life, Jesus spoke with authority from God, not quoting all the rabbis as did the scribes—and as the rishis do (Matt. 7:29).

Holy, complete and without sin, Jesus did not need to strive through endless reincarnations to attain perfection. He was by nature spotless and above reproach. Neither His closest friends nor His enemies could find fault in Him (1 Pet. 1:19,22; 1 John 3:5; Mark 14:55,56).

Jesus had an evenness of vision which did not make good and evil, pleasure and pain, of the same significance or lack of significance. Facing evil in all its stark reality, He resisted temptation, maintaining His integrity and responsible self-control (Matt. 4:-1-11; Heb. 4:15).

But Jesus Christ is more than a teacher and exemplar of a holy life here. He offered His own spotless life an atonement for man's sin. So, unlike the founders of other religions, Jesus came into the world to give His life a *ransom* for others. God the Son came from heaven to put Himself in the place of sinners, to liberate them from the "slave market" of sin. He lovingly suffered the wrath we deserved, offering His own sinless life for our redemption (Mark 10:45; Eph. 1:7).

Yes, the violent death Jesus voluntarily suffered was the *propitiation* for which God could forgive all our sin. Christ's death covers (expiates) the believer's sins and turns away God's righteous wrath against believing sinners (propitiates) (Rom. 3:25; 1 John 2:2).

Christ's death became the ground of *reconciliation* on which the estranged came into fellowship with God. In dying for sinners, Jesus did what no Hindu holy man ever could do for mankind. By bearing the judgment human rebellion against God deserved, Christ provided for a believer's justification before God's moral law, his redemption from the power of selfishness in his life and his reconciliation to fellowship with God from whom he was estranged (2 Cor. 5:18-20; Eph. 2:12-16).

But how do Christians know that all this was provided at the cross? God gave assurance to all men in that He raised Christ from the dead (Acts 17:31). Jesus conquered death itself as ascended to heaven where He has all authority in heaven and earth (Matt. 28:18-20; Eph. 1:20-22).

The great leaders of all other religions die and remain dead. Jesus Christ alone is risen. He alone conquered man's greatest enemies: sin and death. He alone can forgive sin and give eternal life.

In his classic on *The Finality of Christ,* Robert E. Speer argued that "valid experience must rest, even though unconsciously, on truth as well as lead us to truth. Our experience of Christ is valid because it is the experience of a true fact and a real person."[6] Speer observed the inescapable and unique connection between Christ and the gospel.

TM may have its recent origin in a historical personality, but Maharishi asks people to follow his technique, whereas Christ asked people to follow Him. Transcendental meditators hesitate even to be called devotees of the Maharishi, whereas almost from the beginning the disciples were called Christians, realizing at once the appropriateness and inevitableness of the name.

Speer argued that we can still hold the original view of Jesus because "the religious experience of the first Christians, and of all Christians since, has been the experience of Christ, not of the remembrance of Him, nor of imitation of Him, but the actual experience of His living personal Spirit with and in the spirit of the believer. This was Christ's own conception. 'Abide in me and I in you . . . . I am the vine, ye are the branches' " (John 15:4,5, *KJV*).[7]

Charles S. Braden carefully assesses similarities

and differences in *Jesus Compared: A Study of Jesus and Other Great Founders of Religion*. What he says in relation to Krishna, the hero of the *Bhagavad-Gita*, applies not only to Krishna but also to Maharishi:

"So Christ and Krishna stand side by side. One suspects, as the centuries pass and the various cultures of the world interpenetrate ever more deeply, there will be an increasing tendency for them to flow together. This will be resisted by the Christian world, for Christianity . . . has at any given period felt that it was unique, and that it must be kept from mingling with any lesser faith.

"In the process, it seems to one Christian observer, perhaps because of his own Christian background, that Krishna is far more likely to become Christ-like than Jesus to become Krishna-like. Could it be that this is the way in which the fulfillment of the prophecy in Scripture is to be realized—'That every knee shall bow and every tongue confess that Jesus Christ is Lord to the glory of the Father'?"[8] (Phil. 2:10,11).

At present, however, the leader of TM teaches people how to become indistinguishable from abstract Being. Jesus Christ gave Himself that God might remain just and put sinners right with Himself. The one is plain Hinduism; the other Christianity. To acknowledge Maharishi as the teacher of teachers is far from bowing to Jesus as Saviour and Lord of all.

Footnotes

1. Maharishi, *On the Bhagavad-Gita* (VI, 41,42), pp. 460,461.
2. *Ibid.* (VI, 32), pp. 447-50.
3. *Ibid.* (V, 7,18,27), pp. 338,342,344,358,376,377.
4. *Ibid.* (VI, 43,45), pp. 462,464.
5. *Ibid.*, p. 469 for a list of "the cherished names of the great masters of the holy tradition of Vedic wisdom," entitled, "The Holy Tradition."
6. Robert E. Speer, *The Finality of Christ* (Westwood, New Jersey: Fleming H. Revell Company, 1933), p. 202.
7. *Ibid.*, p. 210.
8. Charles S. Braden, *Jesus Compared: A Study of Jesus and Other Great Founders of Religion* (Englewood Cliffs, New Jersey: Prentice-Hall, 1957), p. 72.

5

What Does It Mean to Experience God?

At this point, let us consider the teachings of Maharishi Mahesh Yogi and their relationship to the Hindu and Christian views of what it means to experience God.

The Hindu View: Experiencing God

The ultimate goal of a meditator is not freedom from stress, happiness or additional creativity. It is, like a yogi, to lose his individuality in pure Being. Maharishi writes, "Whatever the mind's experiences during meditation, they are just relative states of the medium of meditation. These states become finer and finer until eventually nothing is left of the medium and the mind is left all by itself in the state of pure consciousness."[1] Since this state is beyond all differentiation nothing can be said about it. The best one can do is to repeat, 'I am That, You are That and all this is That."

And that's that!

As a meditator, did George Harrison achieve TM's ultimate goal of losing his individuality in pure Being? Did the former Beatle ever achieve the state of pure consciousness through meditation upon his mantra? Harrison mentioned that his mantra appeared in Lennon's song, "I Am the Walrus." The first line from the song is "I am he, as you are he, as you are me, and we are all together."[2]

And that is also that!

The goal of meditation is not always stated as the ability to achieve a state of pure consciousness, but often as the freedom to realize one's full potential. But what does that really mean? Do not assume at this point that the connotation you have of your potential is what TM teachers have in mind.

Maharishi says one's full potential "is the unlimited potential of the universal Being."[3] It is not the potential then of your own uniqueness that is realized but of what you have in common with all others, the potential of "isness!" It means, the Maharishi explains, "the unfolding of all the divine in man and bringing the human consciousness to the high pedestal of God-consciousness."[4]

Since God is Being or "isness," we might say it is an experience of isness-consciousness, or of being an "izzard"! Results of this mystical experience of union with Being are traced for thought, speech, action, behavior, health, education, rehabilitation of criminals, recreation, ethics and freedom from fear and tension. But the experience itself is quite different from all of these.

The typical Hindu trilogy is completed when to monistic being and consciousness of unity is added the experience of bliss. When TM propagandists speak of bliss, they mean "concentrated happiness of absolute nature and permanent status. Therefore the art of Being means that the concentrated state of happiness should be constantly lived under all circumstances."[5] In claims like this, TM literature

43

promises people absolute happiness here in this relative and fallen world. TM promises a life that is "blissful, naturally free from suffering, misery, tension, confusion and disharmony."[6]

The ultimate experience of TM may also be called "fulfillment," meaning that fulfillment in the God-conscious life comes when a person is indistinguishable from God. As the Maharishi explains, a person is fulfilled when "the man is the living expression of the omnipresent, omniscient, cosmic existence . . . . The formless appears in form, the silence becomes vibrant, the inexpressible is expressed in personality, and the cosmic life is breathed by the individual."[7] In effect, the individual is absorbed in Brahman (Being) and no longer is distinguishable from "That."

Maharishi puts some very high obligations upon meditators. Each meditator should be righteous and loving "in the inner core of his heart."[8] And this must be developed twenty-four hours of every day.

"It is highly important that a situation should somehow be created in the world that every man is a righteous man. Each man should be a compassionate, loving, and helpful man whose every thought should be kind, loving and virtuous . . . . Each individual should develop his consciousness in such a manner that he is always right and good."[9]

The ideal is great, but one wonders how there can really be a difference between good and evil in a monistic universe. And one wonders what the "somehow" is that will create this dream.

Clearly no one will help a person change the inner core of his heart and become always right and good. Each meditator must transform himself. Maharishi insists, "This may only be created by each individual for himself by transforming the nature of his mind in such a way, and to such an extent, that, by nature, the mind can pick up only right thoughts and engage in right speech and action. Each man has to rise to this state by himself. Nobody else can possibly raise the standard of another's consciousness . . . . Everyone has to work out his own destiny."[10]

Although each person must work out his own destiny, other parts of the TM literature say that the process of meditation is effortless. Meditators are said to be "attracted" to higher levels and move to them naturally. "To go to a field of greater happiness is the natural tendency of the mind."[11]

Because the mind in TM is seeking bliss consciousness, the mind finds that the way is increasingly attractive as it advances in the direction of bliss. So the practice of TM is not only simple but "automatic."[12] A former meditator described it like this, "Let the mind float on the mantra until the conscious mind cannot hold a thought and just drifts off."

Harrison Pope, Jr., a medical student who has spent some years in TM, finds as a result of his interviews with people in the Eastern subcultures that their central theme and purpose is the transformation of the self. The process, he adds, includes three steps: (1) withdrawal from the "establishment" because of its dangers to health and the futility of rebellion; (2) purification from something even more fundamental amiss in the human mind such as stress and anxiety; and (3) enlightenment, achievement of a higher state of consciousness, a state beyond Western knowledge and perhaps immune to scientific probing.[13] Unfortunately, the self-transformation that meditators seek ultimately becomes self-absorption in Brahman, and this is not necessarily "higher."

The Christian View: Experiencing God

Just as the nature of experience is determined by the nature of Being in TM, it is determined by the nature of a personal, transcendent Creator in Christianity. Yet, though one is dependent upon the natural Fatherhood of God for his life and breath, he may be far from the moral and spiritual Fatherhood of God. He may be morally corrupt, spiritually estranged from God and in all justice under condemnation.

Experience of the personal God of the Bible through faith in Jesus Christ as Saviour and Lord is a more radical type of transformation of the self by God. And it begins with repentance for the sin which corrupts not only people in the "establishment," but also all subcultures and anti-establishment groups.

Everyone has sinned (Rom. 3:10-20). Sin is man's greatest problem in every situation. People need to be delivered from sin first; then the resources are available for release from the frustrating quest for lasting peace. But the unforgiven heart is like the restless sea that endlessly casts up mire and dirt (Isa. 57:20,21).

The sinner who becomes identified with Christ by faith is liberated from the curse of karma, of law (Gal. 3:10-13). The Christian believer experiences the inexpressible joy of forgiveness from the penalty of all his sins (1 Pet 1:6-8) and the freedom of a new heart or nature with the power to say "no" to temptation (John 8:34-36).

In Christian experience, dualities between God's existence and man's are not denied. They are very real. And though the loving I/Thou experience never

46

obliterates the difference between Creator and creature, it does reflect acceptance with the living God (Eph. 1:5-8; 1 John 1:3).

The sinner coming to God does not lose his individuality; only his sin. He is liberated from his depravity and reconciled to fellowship with God. In attaining a state of acceptance with God through trusting Christ, he can then accept himself, others and the world as they are without tension (1 John 1:6,7).

Insignificant in the TM experience is the central relationship of Christians to their God—love. "The yearning, if yearning there is, is all for moksa, 'release,' from our wretched conditioned humanity into our true immortal state which is beyond space and time. It is a yearning for a changed condition, not for a Person. In all Indian mystical writing before the *Bhagavad-Gita* . . . there is no trace of love for the deity."[14]

One looks in vain for the priority of love for God and neighbor in TM. Asked what is the first and great commandment, Jesus said, "Love the Lord your God with all your heart, with all your soul, and with all your mind. This is the first and great commandment. And the second is like it: love your neighbor as yourself. All the law and the prophets hang on these two commandments" (Matt. 22:-37-40).

In the Christian new birth, the regenerated person not only loves God and his neighbor, but is renewed in knowledge (Col. 3:10), righteousness and true holiness (Eph. 4:24). After the new birth into spiritual life, the Christian grows. Realization of one's tremendous potential in Christ is gradual throughout life. As believers refuse to yield to selfishness, greed, lust and anger, and yield themselves to the Holy Spirit who dwells within, they become more and more like Christ (2 Cor. 3:17,18).

So Christianity and TM do agree that sinful man needs to become righteous and loving in "the core of his heart." But Christianity further recognizes that a person's highest potential cannot be experienced until he is born from above—supernaturally (2 Cor. 5:-17,18).

As Jesus puts it, "You must be born again" (John 3:3-8). That is the only way in which the Maharishi's goal of becoming righteous and loving in the inner core of his heart can be achieved in God's sight. So the re-created ones do not engage in self-deification, worship of the Brahman-atman within, but in surrender of themselves to their Creator and Redeemer (1 Thess. 1:9,10).

Christianity and TM also agree that a person's being determines his action. But Christianity denies that a sinner can atone for his own sins or change his own nature any more than a leopard can change his spots (Jer. 13:23; John 8:34).

A bad tree must be made good before it can bring forth good fruit (Matt. 7:17,18). But a tree cannot change its own nature. And neither can a person by meditation radically change "the core of his heart" (Jer. 17:9).

It is supernatural power of the Holy Spirit that must give a man new spiritual life. And this is done on the ground of Christ's atonement and according to the grace of God the Father. God Himself gives this life from above through the sinner's faith in Christ's substitutionary sacrifice of Himself for the sins of the world (Eph. 2:8-10).

The sinner alone has not planned the just basis

upon which he could be forgiven, *but* God the Father has. The sinner himself cannot provide the basis for salvation, *but* Christ has. The sinner cannot change his nature, *but* the Holy Spirit gives him this new birth from above.

The Christian makes no claim in this life for an absolute bliss. Yet as a recipient of the grace of the triune God, he possesses a deep and lasting joy, for he anticipates a more direct and glorious experience of God in heaven. Because of God's redemptive love, he enjoys perfect standing in heaven, an assurance of eternal life and, hence, a peace with God that passes understanding (Phil. 4:4-7).

The believer can never again come under condemnation, for he has passed from a state of spiritual death to a state of spiritual life. He need not strive to attain perfection; the perfection of Jesus Christ Himself has been put to his account in heaven. He is justified by faith, not by thousands of lifetimes of striving (Rom. 5:1; 8:1-4).

Meanwhile, as a child of the Creator-Redeemer, as a member of God's moral and spiritual family, the disciple of Christ does not deny the reality of sin (1 John 1:8,10), or shun the challenge of suffering for righteousness' sake in a fallen world (1 Pet. 4:-12-14). Realistically, he faces life with all its problems. In the face of testings and trials, he brings forth the fruit of the Holy Spirit: love, joy, peace, longsuffering, gentleness, kindness, faith, meekness and self-control (Gal. 5:22,23).

The filling of the Holy Spirit does not annihilate the ego, but brings "harmony out of the tension of discordant contents . . . . The psyche is brought to a totally new level of reality . . . . It is made a harmonious part of a total human psyche, which has a new center of focus."[15]

The Christian experiences creative freedom. He is never more free from the bonds of sin than when filled with the Holy Spirit. The fruit of the Holy Spirit is self-control in all of life, including one's thoughts and consciousness.

The Holy Spirit frees the mind to think true thoughts, the emotions to rejoice in that which is good and lovely, and the will to do what is right. All that the Spirit takes from us is the sin which keeps us from growing to the full stature of Christ. Freedom is not arbitrary spontaneity in a vacuum, it is responsible interaction with reality, both divine and human (Gal. 5:1, 13; 1 Pet. 2:16,17).

In contrast to the consciousness of unity in TM, the Christian's consciousness of acceptance with God is based on conceptual truth. An encounter with God does not render meaningless the teaching of Scripture and the words conveying them. Jesus said, "The words that I have spoken unto you are spirit and life" (John 6:63).

Empty words can be legalistic hindrances to a vital experience of God. However, words need not be an end in themselves. They may be vehicles of meaning used by the Holy Spirit to lead a person to the God who is beyond the universe (John 20:31).

Truth is the key to reality. In experiencing God, a believer finds the promises of Scripture to be faithful and true. His richest spiritual experiences build upon the foundation of the words inspired by God; they do not displace those faithful words.

Jesus said, "If you love me, you will keep my commandments" (John 14:15). He also said, "If you continue in my word . . . . you will know the

50

truth, and the truth will make you free" (John 8:31,-32).

Mike, a former meditator for over a year, became frustrated with TM because it promised perfect bliss but did not deliver it. He did experience some initial benefits, he said, but from that point on it was work, work, work, mind-control, mind-control, mind-control.

The theory of a spontaneous attraction from one level of consciousness to the next simply did not represent Mike's experience. In the two years he was in TM he met no one who "had gotten there" through meditation. "It held out a false idealism," he said, "which was never really there."

Then Mike picked up his roommate's copy of the New Testament, *Good News for Modern Man*. The Sermon on the Mount, he found, was what he had been looking for. Christianity was more practical in dealing with real situations.

Mike continued to read Scripture, trusted Christ and found a fulfilling fellowship with God. "A change occurred," he explained, "that I had not created. An outside force changed my life."

Mike had looked to TM to purify his mind. Now through scriptural meditation he found grace to think on things that are true, honorable, just, pure, lovely, gracious, excellent, worthy and praiseworthy (Phil. 4:8).

"If anyone is in Christ, he is a new creation" (2 Cor. 5:17). This is true because Christianity enables a person to find integrity, love and identity as a twice-born child of God, and freedom from the domination of sin. Renewed in the image of God and following the example of Jesus Christ, the devotee of Christ

51

shares the eternal purposes of God for life as it is lived once for all in its brief span on earth.

The Christian senses the urgency of his mission since people's destiny is settled here and now. He finds an awesome responsibility as he stands before people in the place of Christ pleading with them to be reconciled to God. In a daily walk with God, in trusting obedience, he finds all the challenge the highest values in life can give.

In sum, TM offers an experience involving the loss of one's distinctive identity, a realization of one's indistinguishability from abstract Being, perfect bliss and fulfillment in a monistic sense, the demand for perfect righteousness by one's own graceless effort. The essential self-transformation that people seek in TM, however, turns out to eliminate the self.

In contrast, Christianity offers an experience in which the I/Thou duality remains and the fallen self is regenerated from above. Through the surrender of repentant faith one enjoys forgiveness, redemption and reconciliation. Foremost in the Christian's relation to God and others is love—*agapé*. A person realizes his own unique potential, deep joy and creative freedom through Spirit-illumined truth.

The experience TM promotes turns out to be religious rather than scientific. It offers a Hindu type of self-salvation, not simply a technique of health and education. It is difficult indeed to see how it can be taught in public schools as nonreligious or how Christians can maintain their faith with integrity, if they practice TM with any understanding of its significance. What happens to the self in the one case— absorption into Being—is impossible of realization if the distinctness of the self is retained, regenerated, sanctified and finally glorified.

52

Robert Brow, who lived in India for twenty years, concluded, "Obviously if God is merely a World Soul or the life principle of the universe, then a sense of merging with this principle is all man can aspire to. If, on the other hand, God is supremely personal, and wants man to be supremely personal and to know and love Him, then the monistic experience is personality suicide. Those who know the God of Abraham, and David, and Isaiah, and Paul, and John, can deny neither their own significance as persons, nor the distinctive personality of the God whom they serve."[16]

Footnotes

1. Maharishi, *Transcendental Meditation*, p. 55.
2. Cited by Bob Larson, *Hippies, Hindus and Rock and Roll* (Carol Stream, Illinois: Creation House, 1972), p. 42.
3. Maharishi, *Transcendental Meditation*, p. 80.
4. *Ibid.*, pp. 137-141.
5. *Ibid.*, p. 101.
6. *Ibid.*
7. *Ibid.*, pp. 248,249.
8. *Ibid.*, pp. 88,89.
9. *Ibid.*, pp. 72,73.
10. *Ibid.*, p. 73.
11. *Ibid.*, p. 49.
12. *Ibid.*, p. 50.
13. Harrison Pope, Jr., *The Road East: America's New Discovery of Eastern Wisdom* (Boston: Beacon Press, 1974), pp. 135-139).
14. R. C. Zaehner, *Hindu and Muslim Mysticism* (New York: Schocken Books, 1969), p. 11.
15. Morton Kelsey, *Encounter with God* (Minneapolis, Minn.: Bethany Fellowship, 1972), p. 165.
16. Taken from *Religion: Origins and Ideas* by Robert Brow. © Inter-Varsity Fellowship, London. Used by permission from InterVarsity Press, U.S.A.

6

What Is the Way
to an Experience of God?

Let us consider finally the teachings of Maharishi Mahesh Yogi and their relationship to Hindu and Christian views of the way to get an experience of the Source.

The Hindu View:
The Way to Experiencing God

According to Maharishi, the process of bringing the attention to the level of the transcendental Being is known as "the system of transcendental deep meditation." In this process, "a proper thought in its infant state of development enables the conscious mind to arrive systematically at the source of thought, the field of Being. Thus the way to experience the transcendental Being lies in selecting a proper thought and experiencing its subtle states until its subtlest state is experienced and transcended."[1]

More than the content of the thought is at work in TM, for thoughts are said to have vibrations. Thinking is considered to be a subtle form of speech, and thought a subtle form of sound. Since the ultimate Reality is beyond thought, it is reasoned, the clue to transcendence may be the vibrations rather than the content.

"The influence of a spoken word that is carried by the waves of vibrations in the atmosphere does not depend upon the meaning of the word. It lies in the quality of the vibrations that are set forth. Therefore, where it is necessary to produce vibrations of good quality that produce an influence of harmony and happiness, it also is necessary that the quality of the vibration should correspond to that of the individual."[2]

People, as well as thoughts and words, are held to emit distinctive vibrations. Individuals differ in the quality of their vibrations as they differ in personality. "That is why the selection of a proper thought for a particular individual is a vital factor in the practice of transcendental deep meditation."[3]

Devotees of TM receive a secret mantra. Trained masters of meditation at the TM centers assign a certain mantra to correspond with the special quality of the individual. According to one meditator converted to Christ, there are some seven types of personalities and corresponding mantras.

The mantras are actually meaningless sounds or "words" that produce certain effects. One convert said his secret word was *Iyim*. This "word" was to be repeated whenever his mind wandered to concrete thoughts. Thus his mind was cleansed and directed again to Being itself, which is beyond all thoughts.

The goal of the meditator is God-consciousness or Unity with the Impersonal God. To this end, he engages in simple repetition of his secret mantra twenty minutes each morning and evening—TM in the AM and the PM! This practice leads ultimately to a state of Unity, a state of consciousness without any specific content, with no specifiable objects or subjects. All differentiations allegedly cease when the vibrations of the meditator unite indistinguishably with the vibrations of the Absolute.

Many people begin TM without understanding the Hindu philosophy of religion behind it, but that philosophy governs the method nevertheless. And the advanced meditator reading the Yogi's books will eventually adopt his Hindu philosophy.

A prospective devotee who cares to understand what is going on in TM must be able to convince himself, along with the Maharishi, that the observable world is neither real nor unreal. When Maharishi sees a tree, he cannot say the tree is unreal, but he does say it is always changing.

As he looks at a tree, the Maharishi reasons in this way:

"Because it is always changing it is not real, but because it is there, for all practical purposes, we have to credit the tree with the status of existence. . . . We call it 'phenomenal existence.' The phenomenon of the tree is there, even though it is not real. . . . The conclusion is that the world is neither real nor unreal."[4] In other words, the tree is a mirage.

Changing the analogy, "The many forms of phenomena of the world around are like the ripples and the waves, a mirage that only appears to exist in the unbounded existence of God."[5] This basic presupposition underlies the most simple and secular statements of the TM method, whether a meditator wants to acknowledge it or not.

There can be no question that even the technique of TM is characteristic of Hinduism. The Maharishi extols the fact that it is derived from the *Bhagavad-Gita,* the most exalted of Hindu sacred writings. In his extensive commentary on this Hindu writing, Maharishi exclaims, "The *Bhagavad-Gita* is the Light of Life, lit by God at the altar of man to save humanity from the darkness of ignorance and suffering. . . . The *Bhagavad-Gita* is a complete guide to practical life. . . . It brings fulfillment to the life of the individual.

"When society accepts it, social well-being and security will result, and when the world hears it, world peace will be permanent. . . . It surpasses any practical wisdom of life ever cherished by human society. . . .

"The *Bhagavad-Gita* is the scripture of Yoga, the scripture of Divine Union. Its purpose is to explain in theory and practice all that is needed to raise the consciousness of man to the highest possible level."[6]

Clearly, then, the Maharishi's method of attaining divine unity is a Hindu method derived from the major Hindu scripture. However secular the terminology employed by American teachers of SCI and TM, Maharishi knows that the method itself is one of the ways to self-elimination taught in Hindu scripture.

The Christian View:
The Way to Experiencing God

The Christian way to an experience of God differs radically from the TM way to absorption in Brahman. The Christian way leads to loving fellowship with the personal transcendent Lord of the Bible.

The Bible is the Christian Scriptures and the primary source of knowledge for the believer. It is the Bible which presents Jesus as the way, the truth and the life without which none can come to the Father. (See John 14:6.)

The Bible did not originate by the mere impulse of

57

man, but by men who carried along by the Holy Spirit, spoke from God (2 Peter 1:21). Therefore, all Scripture is inspired of God and profitable. It is the Bible that God inspired which gives people the knowledge essential to reconcile them to God and to equip them for every good work (2 Tim. 3:15-17).

Consciousness of the God of the Bible involves awareness of truth revealed in the biblical writings about Him and His purposes. God is distinct from, but not totally different than the human mind. God created man's mind to think His thoughts after Him (Col. 3:10). And it is by the content of Scripture that the Christian's mind is directed to the God who transcends being itself.

When a person places his faith in Christ the Holy Spirit renews him in his capacity to grow in conceptual knowledge of God. This truth guides a believer away from empty idols and demonic powers, and to the living God.

The Christian does not seek to transcend all thoughts, but to worship both spirit and truth (see John 4:24). He sings, prays and testifies with the Spirit, but with the understanding also, for in the deepest spiritual experiences, the mind is not to be unfruitful. (See 1 Cor. 14:13-19.)

The Christian's confidence and hope do not rest upon a repetition of meaningless sounds or mantras, nor upon alleged vibrations of words or thoughts, harmonious or otherwise. Neither does the biblical way to an experience of God require a denial of the plain facts of change and diversity.

Experiencing God through Jesus Christ does not suggest that one persuades himself he is divine, for to confuse oneself with Deity is not deep spirituality, but deep idolatry. Christians neither deify self nor despise self.

Christians do not regard the world either as ultimate Reality or as a mere mirage. Christians find no need to persuade themselves of the unreality of that for which there is adequate evidence. Knowing that God has created all things, Christians are open to any material or spiritual reality for which sufficient evidence exists. They do not try to escape reality, but accept it from God. Having met the living God, Christians have no need for inventing a permanent reality and convincing themselves of it by anything like "self-hypnosis."

It is in order that men should avoid such speculations as TM induces that God gave a reliable, written revelation of Himself through inspired authors. The content of that thought—not meaningless sounds—is the key to religious reality (Rom. 10:1,2,11,17).[7]

The gospel of Jesus Christ informs the mind of the fact that God became man, and that eyewitnesses confirmed accounts of Jesus' life, death and resurrection (1 Cor. 15:5-8; 1 John 1:1-3). It summons people to believe these facts (Luke 24:46,47). It also informs of God's eternal purposes through Christ's death: to save sinners (1 Cor. 15:3,4).

Whatever may be the case of people's alleged vibrations, all men are sinners in need of a Saviour. Consequently, the hope of sinners for liberation from their sin is in the publicly confirmed gospel of Christ, not in a secret mantra without meaning. So God summons men to believe that Christ died for their sins. And the gospel calls upon sinners to commit themselves to the living Christ as Saviour and Lord. One who responds to these facts and their meaning, and trusts Christ Himself, receives life: eternal fellowship with the Father and the Son through the Spirit (John 3:36; 5:24).[8]

Belief of the biblical message brings with it, as J.B. Phillips and countless others have found, "The Ring of Truth." And through Spirit-illumined Scripture, a sinner not only comes to Christ, but grows in Him as he grows in the knowledge of God's Word (2 Pet. 1:3-8).

As you study what the Bible says about meditation, you find that the motivation behind it is not just a desire for what it can do for you, but rather a love for God Himself. And so a Christian cries out with the Psalmist, "O how I love thy law! it is my meditation all the day" (Ps. 119:97).

Remember, it is a believer's purpose, among other things, to be pleasing to God in thought. So if you are a believer being drawn to TM, I urge you to pray, "Let the words of my mouth, and the meditation of my heart, be acceptable in thy sight, O Lord, my strength, and my redeemer" (Ps. 19:14, *KJV*).

One can be assured that he is thinking proper thoughts when he meditates upon God's statutes, precepts, commandments, law testimonies and promises (Ps. 119:15,23,48,78,97,99,148). Every reader would do well to study Psalm 119 for himself.

The New Testament emphasis is similar. Paul says to young Timothy, "Until I come, devote yourself to the public reading of Scripture, to preaching and to teaching. Do not neglect your gift. . . . Be diligent in these matters; give yourself wholly to them, so that everyone may see your progress. Watch your life and doctrine closely. Persevere in them, because if you do, you will save both yourself and your hearers" (1 Tim. 4:13-16, *NIV*).

Christians guide their meditation with Scripture in

different ways. One method includes the following steps:

1. *Feel the need.* We can never live by bread alone (Matt. 4:4). Our inner nature must be renewed day by day (2 Cor. 4:16).

2. *Enjoy the quest.* Capture the expectation and excitement of discovering for yourself a scripturally guided experience with God and others. Explore new ways to express your love for God and neighbor. Consider creative ways to live a holy life. "Blessed are those who hunger and thirst for righteousness" (Matt. 5:6).

3. *Read a paragraph.* Longer sections of Scripture may contain too many ideas for adequate response and application in one day. A single verse without its context may be misinterpreted. For devotional purposes, one unit of thought is sufficient. Study the paragraph in an unmarked translation or compare translations.

4. *State its meaning.* Requesting the guidance of the Holy Spirit who inspired the Bible, determine the primary teaching of the paragraph. Does it state, imply or illustrate a general principle? What did the writer intend to teach the first readers?

We need not look for hidden, "deeper" meanings. In the name of "getting a blessing," fantastic ideas have been read into the Bible. No teaching of Scripture is too simple or mundane to be profitable. To think God's thoughts after Him with precision, write out the paragraph's basic teaching.[9]

5. *Reflect upon it.* Memorize the key phrase or verse, so that you can repeat it day and night. Visualize its meaning, underline its importance for you, explore its implications and trace its relationships to other truths of Scripture. Appreciate its significance

and make it a part of you. If you can sing, express it in song.

6. *Apply it personally.* Although the original meaning was one, the present applications are many. Apply the teaching to your own life by using personal references (I, me, my), immediate time references (this morning, today, now), and specific roles you fill (friend, student, teacher, husband, wife, father, mother, son, daughter, etc.). For example, "I today as husband, father, teacher, colleague and citizen will reflect my joy in the Lord" (Phil. 4:4).

7. *Commit yourself to it.* What God desires must make a difference in your spirit, plans and purposes. Having discovered God's will, yield to it completely. Pray as Jesus did, "not as I will, but as Thou wilt" (Matt. 26:39).

8. *Act on it.* The best intentions are not sufficient. By the Spirit of grace be a doer of the Word and not a hearer only (James 1:22; Matt. 7:21-27). Look for opportunities during the day to put the principle into practice. Those who walk in the truth (light) have fellowship with the Father, with His Son and one another so that their joy is complete (1 John 1:-3-7).[10]

9. *Pray about it.*

By comparison, the richly varied experience of Christians in fellowship with their personal Creator-Saviour-Counselor makes a spiritual experience narrowly limited to contentless vibrations seem deprived indeed. Christian prayer is a many-splendored relationship of response and request to the Lord of all revealed supremely in the Christ of history and the truths of Scripture.

In response to God's gracious initiatives, the believer expresses his faith in worship, confession, adoration, praise, thanksgiving and dedicated action. Furthermore, the Christian may meaningfully offer intercession for others and petitions for himself to a personal Lord who hears and wisely responds to sincere petition. How improverished is the spiritual experience of one whose Source is impersonal and whose experience is limited to mere "meditation."[11]

Can one practice TM to deepen his devotional life and remain an active Christian? Listen to the experience of a young man named Roy. After his initiation into TM and first meditations, he experienced an unusual mental alertness.

Coming from a small mountain town, he had previously found the streets of Denver very confusing. But after the meditation he "saw" them clearly and found his way around easily. He experienced the rest and relaxation promised, and his sinus problems ceased.

A nominal Christian, Roy decided to read the Bible and ask God to show him if his TM experiences were of God. As he studied the first five booklets in the Navigator series on Christianity he sensed his need of the Saviour and late one night received Christ into his life.

After his conversion to Christ he noticed some problems with meditating. His meditations, he said, became "ragged." And the Christian life did not seem to be all that it should be.

Roy attended a week-end retreat sponsored by TM, ate the vegetarian diet, meditated and did the exercises to use up the stored energy and overcome the lethargy from the meditation. Instead of strengthening him in TM, this week-end posed further problems for him.

At the suggestion of his pastor, and with the help

of an exhaustive concordance, Roy studied everything the Bible had to say about meditation. He came to see that the biblical approach to meditation and the TM approach were not the same. A real "hassle" occurred between them in his mind.

He checked out his meditating procedure in Colorado Springs and was assured he was doing it right. However, after that he determined to cease doing TM and meditate only upon the truth of Scripture. Since that time, he said. *"I have had everything TM promises and more!"* Roy now thinks that TM was a deceptive means of making him feel that he had the proper way to God, when he did not, and it kept him from the abundant life Christ came to give.

Any Christian involved with TM should study Scripture on meditation and pray as Roy did, "Lord, if TM is of you, bless it; if it is not, help me to put it away."

Footnotes

1. Maharishi, *Transcendental Meditation*, p. 46.
2. *Ibid.*, p. 51.
3. *Ibid.*
4. *Ibid.*, p. 276.
5. *Ibid.*, p. 283.
6. Maharishi, *On the Bhagavad-Gita*, pp. 19,20.
7. Gordon R. Lewis, "God's Word: Key to Authentic Spirituality," ed. Bruce Shelley, *A Call to Christian Character* (Grand Rapids: Zondervan, 1970), pp. 105-120.
8. See John Stott, *Basic Christianity* (Downers Grove, Illinois: InterVarsity Press, 1965), 144 pp. for a clear presentation of the central Christian message.
9. On interpreting Scripture see T. Norton Sterrett, *How to Understand Your Bible* (Downers Grove, Ill.: InterVarsity Press, 1974), pp. 1-179.
10. Compare steps in meditation by A.J. Appasamy, *What Shall We Believe?* (Post Box 501, Madras 3, India: The Christian Literature Society, 1971), pp. 32-35. (1) Be still, (2) Listen to God (What is the message you wanted to teach Isaiah? What is the message you are giving me?), (3) Draw a picture clearly in your mind, (4) Turn your thoughts to prayer, (5) Obey fully, change your life, correct your mistakes, practice virtues or engage in significant activities, (6) Keep regular hours for meditation, with discipline studying the Bible as daily spiritual food.
11. For a development of the Christian's view of prayer, see Gordon R. Lewis, "Prayer," ed. Merrill C. Tenney, *The Zondervan Pictorial Encyclopedia of the Bible* (Grand Rapids: Zondervan, 1975) IV, pp. 835-844.

7

What About the TM Experience?

All right, you say, TM may not be Christian in its approach to God, man's need or the way to meet it, but how do you account for the beneficial experiences of Maharishi and his followers?

The experience of which TM writers speak is any one or more of the following possibilities:

1. Deceptive self-hypnosis;
2. Simple self-deification;
3. Non-Redemptive natural religion;
4. Demonic deception.

Self-Hypnosis

One of the most plausible explanations of the TM experience was given by the Maharishi himself when discussing the intellectual way to enlightenment. He explained that contemplation of the perishability of nature leads to interest in an unchanging reality behind the surface of nature. And he called this experience of TM self-hypnosis!

"As his practice of contemplation continues, his mind begins to be established more and more in the eternal Being as his own self. He contemplates in terms of 'I am That,' 'Thou are That,' and 'All this is

That'. . . . Such a state of mind is created in him, that it is as if he has been deeply hypnotized by the notion. . . .

"His consciousness is captured by the idea of oneness of life, and the obvious diversity of existence and phenomenal creation begins to lose its hold. This is the beginning of the experience of the transcendental reality on the level of intellectual understanding. . . . This path of enlightenment is, we could say, a path of self-hypnotism."[1]

Those are the Maharishi's own words!

Self-Deification

Another naturalistic explanation of the TM experience is given by Dr. R. C. Zaehner, professor of Eastern Religions and Ethics at Oxford University:

"It is possible to 'become Brahman' without for that reason entering into loving communion with God; and this is, in fact, what the monistic mystics do. Divested as they are of all their moral trappings they are content to rest in the quiet contemplation of their own souls; having reached the immortal they can conceive of nothing beyond. They are blinded by their own self-sufficiency, for having conquered desire they cannot rekindle desire itself and direct it to its proper goal which is God."[2]

In a chapter of his book headed "Self-Deification," Zaehner charges Hindus with worshiping themselves rather than God:

"In Hindu terminology he (Abu Yazid) sees himself not only as Brahman but as Isvara too, so he has no scruple in exclaiming, 'I am the Lord Most High,' or more preposterously still: 'Verily, I am—there is no God but me, so worship me.' "[3]

Since there is no "Other" with whom to have religious experience, Zaehner further argues, "If the soul is regarded as either being identical with Brahman or as so constituted as to be unable to commune with other souls, then its final fulfillment will not be an ecstasy of union but an 'en-stasy' of introverted narcissism."[4]

Non-Redemptive Natural Religion

Any elements of truth in TM may reflect a transcendence of abstract being and an awareness through nature of the living God's existence and creative power. The Lord of all has disclosed His glory in His handiwork (Ps. 19:1). The existence and greatness of the world attests His existence and power (Rom. 1:18-20).[5]

True knowledge of God may be suppressed and distorted in the ultimate concern of Hindus and the Maharishi for a non-personal abstract being. While fallen men know the Creator, they worship and serve the creature more (Rom. 1:25).

Naturalistic mysticism gives its ultimate concern to the natural religious consciousness and human feelings. It refuses to recognize the external authority of biblical revelation. It will not judge its experience by the normative revelation of God in Scripture. Rather, it judges Scripture by its own religious experience.

As Paul shows in Romans 1—3 there is nothing redemptive in natural religion. Natural religion, B. B. Warfield explains, "grows out of the recognized relations of creature and Maker; it is the creature's response to the perception of its Lord, in feelings of dependence and responsibility. It knows nothing of salvation."

Natural religion fails, Warfield argues, just because it is "unequal to unnatural conditions." It requires to be "supplemented by elements which are proper to the relation of the offering creature to the offended Lord. This is what Christianity brings."

In bringing the gospel to sinners Christianity "so supplements and transforms natural religion as to make it a religion for sinners. It does not supersede natural religion; it takes it up in its entirety unto itself, expanding it, and developing it on new sides to meet new needs and supplementing it where it is insufficient for these new needs."[6]

The issue is further sharpened as Warfield concludes, "The issue which mysticism creates is thus just the issue of Christianity. The question which it raises is, whether we need, whether we have, a provision in the blood of Christ for our sins; or whether we, each of us, possess within ourselves all that can be required for time and for eternity."[7]

Demonic Deception

A further possible explanation of the TM experience remains. Roy alluded to it previously. When anyone opens his mind to whatever influence comes along, he must realize that Satan may offer a deceptively pleasurable "religious" experience.

The purposes of spiritualists at seances is remarkably similar to those of meditators. Raphael Gasson, a former medium, explains that in a student's first sessions he learns "to relax his body and to keep his mind on one thing until he has reached a state of what could be regarded as self-hypnosis and passivity, which results in his not thinking for himself. He becomes an automaton through which evil spirits work by taking advantage of his passivity."[8]

It is very possible that Satan could use the advantages in TM to make a person feel satisfied while

69

bypassing the cross and personal fellowship with the Lord of the universe. Christians are to exercise self-control, not open their minds to the demonic powers.

So TM propaganda must be considered in the light of Maharishi's explanation that it may be self-hypnotism, Zaehner's that it may be self-deification, the apostle Paul's that it may be worship and service of the creature more than the Creator, and Satan's deceptive power to change himself into an angel of light.

Footnotes

1. Maharishi, *Transcendental Meditation*, pp. 278,279.
2. R.C. Zaehner, *Hindu and Muslim Mysticism* (New York: Schocken Books, 1969), p. 15.
3. *Ibid.*, p. 114.
4. *Ibid.*, p. 11.
5. For a biblical study of divine revelation in nature see my *Decide for Yourself* (Downers Grove, Illinois: InterVarsity Press, 1970), pp. 15-19.
6. Benjamin B. Warfield, "Mysticism and Christianity," *Biblical and Theological Studies* (Nutley, New Jersey: Presbyterian and Reformed, 1952), pp. 455,456.
7. *Ibid.*, p. 462.
8. Raphael Gasson, *The Challenging Counterfeit* (Plainfield, New Jersey: Logos Books, 1966), p. 83.

8

What About the Claims of TM?

Transcendental Meditation claims to be "a scientific technique for health and education." It is much more than that.

A Total World and Life View

First of all, an understanding of the most secular expressions of the method derived from the Maharishi Mahesh Yogi's writings shows that it involves a whole world view and way of life. Any use of TM with understanding of its import involves the meditator in this philosophy of life.

William Johnston acknowledges that meditation may be done for non-religious motives—relief of tension or acumen in business, but he points out that many of the self-styled agnostic meditators are religiously motivated because they are searching for truth. "And sooner or later, if they continue their practice, they will be confronted with ultimate questions of life and death and faith and the Absolute."[1] Over the long run, meditators cannot avoid the implications of their technique.

A Hindu Religious Practice

Second, the evidence we have already examined demonstrates the fact that the world view and way of life inherent in the SCI/TM technique is a religious, not a secular perspective. Maharishi himself acknowledges the Hindu sources. TM is essentially Hindu religious practice.

An Unrealistic Outlook

Third, it has been shown that the outlook on reality in SCI/TM is in conflict with the nature of reality as taught in Christianity. No one can, without contradicting himself and the facts of the matter, seriously affirm both TM and Christian views of man's Source, man's basic need, the role of the Maharishi and of Christ in meeting that need, the nature of experiencing God, and the way to that experience.

A Contradiction of Christianity

Fourth, it has become evident that the differences between TM and Christianity are not merely verbal or intellectual. There is a real difference between the monistic and dualistic views of reality and morality. There is a real difference between viewing history as "maya" or as a vital arena of life and action possessing a once-for-all significance for one's eternal destiny.

There is a real difference between allegiance to the Maharishi as the teacher of teachers and allegiance to Jesus Christ as Lord of all. There is a real difference between self-absorption into abstract Being and personal regeneration and eternal fellowship with a personal Lord. There is a real difference between self-justification through self-effort in meditation,

72

and justification by grace through the hearing and receiving of the gospel of Jesus Christ.

A Dangerous Exercise

Writing on meditation in several Eastern forms, William Johnston's, *Silent Music: The Science of Meditation*[1] includes a chapter entitled "A Perilous Journey." Although favorable to meditation—judging it worth the risk, he begins, "If travel in outer space is fraught with danger, in such wise that we need intrepid astronauts, even more perilous is the inner journey into the caverns of the mind."[2] TM propaganda seldom mentions such dangers.

Johnston who has a degree in mystical theology and has taught for the last twenty years in Tokyo warns of two psychological dangers or snares that confront both the psychic explorer and mystic:

"The first is flight from reality, withdrawal into one's own world; the escape syndrome. The second is too rapid or premature entry into higher states of consciousness."[3]

Inability to control and integrate mystical experiences may lead to neglect of the outer world and so to schizophrenia.

"Because of the great perils involved, most religious traditions have sought to initiate their devotees into mystical silence rather than allowed them to wander freely into the deeper caverns of the mind."[4] With all of its check points, TM prides itself on the ease of the free-floating mind toward whatever attracts it!

"All religious traditions know of a mysticism of evil. I remember being shocked when I first heard of a 'samadhi' of pure evil." Because of a possible bad meditative "trip" traditional mysticism required an

73

aspiring meditator to have "undergone a conversion and be totally dedicated to good."[5] Do the teachers of TM take this precaution?

Meditation is a snare if the experiences it brings are made an end in themselves. If one "clings to them as if they were absolutes" he sticks there and makes no progress.[6]

The development of insight, intuitive power and even extra-sensory perception may become a dangerous fascination distracting the mystic from his true goal which is "wisdom in emptiness, the all which is nothing."[7]

Furthermore, Johnston warns, "If all power fascinates and corrupts, how much more fascinating and corrupting is the lure of psychic power over the minds of other men! This is a terrible temptation."[8]

As indicated above, one may open himself to the influence of demons. Dr. Elmer Green of the Menninger Clinic said, "According to various warnings, the persistent explorer in these realms . . . brings himself to the attention of indigenous beings, who, under normal circumstances, pay little attention to humans . . . . They are of many natures and some are malicious, cruel and cunning."[9]

The experiences may in the psychologist's terms be maladaptive or harmful. Certain states in false mysticism, Johnston continues, are undesirable because they are "irrelevant or morbid or regressive, or because they lead away from reality and wisdom, or because they lead to evil or self-glorification or to destruction or to hatred. All of which are real possibilities."[10]

Admittedly, these aberrations are "well-known" in the history of any evolving religion. Discernment is difficult because you seldom if ever, find one-

74

hundred-per-cent true mysticism. "Even in the greatest mystics one finds elements of self-deception or illusion as well as emotional disturbances and the ordinary mental sickness to which mortal man is heir."[11]

Christianity has criteria by which to discern the spirits.[12] But what are they in TM when all concepts, consistency, empirical fit and existential relevance is left behind?

Footnotes

1. William Johnston, *Silent Music: The Science of Meditation* (New York: Harper & Row, 1974), p. 20.
2. *Ibid.*, p. 92.
3. *Ibid.*, p. 93.
4. *Ibid.*, p. 94.
5. *Ibid.*, p. 95.
6. *Ibid.*, p. 97.
7. *Ibid.*
8. *Ibid.*, p. 98.
9. Cited in *Ibid.*, pp. 98,99.
10. *Ibid.*, p. 100.
11. *Ibid.*
12. Gordon R. Lewis, "Criteria for Discerning Spirits," ed. John Warwick Montgomery, *Demon Possession,* (Minneapolis: Bethany Fellowship, 1975).

9

What Are the Challenges of TM?

The challenges of TM vary according to the interest and viewpoint of the party being challenged. Nevertheless, the challenges are there, and they are very real.

The Challenge to Leaders of TM

The public relations approach of SCI/TM teachers is less than candid when it claims that TM is not a religion or philosophy, but a technique for doing less and accomplishing more. TM is practiced for the express purpose of leading one back to his Source. And that Source is plainly the Hindu Absolute, Brahman.

The method for reaching that abstract Being is a Hindu method with a long tradition in India. And the Maharishi's writings are a form of Hinduism. These assertions are already abundantly documented in this book.

I call upon SCI/TM officials to identify their product for what it is—Hinduism!

The Challenge to Christians

Because of (1) the obvious Hindu religious implications essential to TM, and (2) its contradictions of the essential teachings of Christianity, already documented in this book, I call upon Christians to refrain from seeking to deepen their devotional lives by taking the secret initiation ceremony and repeating a secret mantra. Rather, let Christians yield to the Holy Spirit's teaching through the Bible's revealed truth in daily, meaningful devotions.

True, it has yet to be shown scientifically that Christian meditation may produce even greater and psychological benefits than TM. Yet who really knows what God could do with even one Christian faithfully practicing the biblical ways to peace, joy, freedom and creativity?

By God's abundant grace let every Christian increasingly realize the tremendous resources for these blessings in a Christlike way!

The Challenge to Every U.S. Citizen

According to the October, 1973 issue of *Nations Schools* magazine, "at least a dozen high schools" offer SCI courses. And "the list keeps growing." In view of the inescapable Hindu religious and philosophical assumptions which underlie SCI/TM teachings, I challenge American citizens and taxpayers to oppose and cease supporting such religious courses as these in their public schools and colleges.

If the United States Constitution forbids a simple Christian prayer—which also has psychological benefits and has kept many people from drug abuse, then it also forbids a simple Hindu method of diverting consciousness from observable reality and conceptual content to Brahman, the alleged ultimate Source of thought.

Whether courses are already approved, as in Illinois, or whether proposals for them are being considered, taxpayers not interested in supporting a type of Hinduism in the nation's public school classrooms should strenuously oppose the use of their money for this purpose. I therefore call upon all citizens to use every means of influence available to them to protest the use of their tax dollars for the teaching of SCI/TM in all public institutions.

This violation of the separation of church and state must not become more entrenched. There is still time to do something about it. Write your congressman and senators on both state and federal levels. Write the members of your school boards.

It will be inexcusable to do too little too late!

About the Author

Gordon R. Lewis, professor of systematic theology and Christian philosophy at Conservative Baptist Theological Seminary, Denver, Colorado, attended Baptist Bible Seminary and Cornell University, and earned an A.B. degree at Gordon College (1948), an M.Div. degree at Faith Theological Seminary (1951) and M.A. and Ph.D. degrees at Syracuse University (1953 and 1959 respectively).

Before joining the faculty of the Denver Seminary in 1958, he served as professor of apologetics and philosophy at Baptist Bible Seminary for seven years and as pastor of People's Baptist Church, Hamilton Park, Delaware, for two years. While teaching he has held a number of interim pastorates in New York and Colorado.

Professor Lewis' articles have appeared in several Christian periodicals and scholarly journals. His three previous books are entitled *Confronting the Cults; Decide for Yourself: A Theological Workbook;* and *Judge for Yourself: A Workbook on Contemporary Challenges to Christian Faith.*

In 1973 he served as visiting professor of theology at Union Biblical Seminary, Yeotmal, India, and visited Christian schools in some ten other Eastern countries.

Bibliography

Anderson, J.N.D. *Christianity and Comparative Religion*. Downers Grove, Illinois: InterVarsity Press, 1970.

Appasamy, A.J. *What Shall We Believe?* India: The Christian Literature Society, 1971.

Braden, Charles S. *Jesus Compared*. Englewood Cliffs, N.J.: Prentice-Hall, Inc., 1957.

Braden, William. *The Private Sea*. Chicago: Quadrangle Books, 1967.

Brow, Robert. *Religion: Origin and Ideas*. Chicago: InterVarsity Press, 1966.

Campbell, Anthony. *Seven States of Consciousness*. New York: Harper & Row, 1974.

Carnell, Edward John. *Christian Commitment: An Apologetic*. New York: The Macmillan Company, 1957.

Carnell, Edward John. *A Philosophy of the Christian Religion*. Grand Rapids: Wm. B. Eerdmans, 1952.

Ebon, Martin, ed. *Maharishi, The Guru*. New York: The New American Library, 1968.

Fisher, David, and Robbins, Jhan. *Tranquility Without Pills*. New York: Bantam Books, 1972.

Forem, Jack. *Transcendental Meditation.* New York: E.P. Dutton & Co., Inc., 1974.

Gasson, Raphael. *The Challenging Counterfeit.* Plainfield, N.J.: Logos Books, 1966.

Guinness, Os. *The Dust of Death.* Downers Grove, Ill.: InterVarsity Press, 1973.

Johnston, William. *Silent Music.* New York: Harper & Row, 1974.

Jones, E. Stanley. *Victory Through Surrender.* Nashville: Abingdon Press, 1966.

Kelsey, Morton. *Encounter with God.* Minneapolis: Bethany Fellowship, Inc., 1972.

Khan, Jordan C. *Life More Abundant.* India: Evangelical Literature Service, 1972.

Krishna, Paul. *Journey from the East.* Downers Grove, Ill.: InterVarsity Press, 1971.

Larson, Bob. *Hippies, Hindus and Rock and Roll.* Carol Stream, Ill.: Creation House, 1972.

Lewis, C.S. *Miracles.* New York: The Macmillan Company, 1948.

Lewis, Gordon R. *Confronting the Cults.* Nutley, N.J.: Presbyterian and Reformed, 1966.

Lewis, Gordon R. *Decide for Yourself: A Theological Workbook.* Downers Grove, Ill.: InterVarsity Press, 1970.

Lewis, Gordon R. *Judge for Yourself: A Workbook on Contemporary Challenges to Christian Faith.* Downers Grove, Ill.: InterVarsity Press, 1974.

Pope, Harrison, Jr. *The Road East: America's New Discovery of Eastern Wisdom.* Boston: Beacon Press, 1974.

Prior, K.F.W. *The Way of Holiness.* Chicago: InterVarsity Press, 1967.

Schaeffer, Francis A. *The New Super-Spirituality.* Downers Grove, Ill.: InterVarsity Press, 1972.

Schaeffer, Francis A. *True Spirituality*. Wheaton, Ill.: Tyndale House, 1971.

Shelley, Bruce, ed. *A Call to Christian Character*. Grand Rapids: Zondervan, 1970.

Stott, John R.W. *Your Mind Matters*. Downers Grove, Ill.: InterVarsity Press, 1972.

Trueblood, Elton. *The Validity of the Christian Mission*. New York: Harper & Row, 1972.

Warfield, Benjamin B. *Biblical and Theological Studies*. Philadelphia: Presbyterian and Reformed, 1952.

Yisudas, G. D. *Are All Religions the Same?* Bombay, India: Gospel Literature Service. 1968.

Yisudas, G.D. *One God Many Manifestations*. Bombay, India: Gospel Literature Service, 1969.

Yogi, Maharishi Mahesh. *Meditations of Maharishi Mahesh Yogi*. New York: Bantam Books, 1968.

Yogi, Maharishi Mahesh. *On the Bhagavad-Gita*. Baltimore, Md.: Penguin Books, 1967.

Yogi, Maharishi Mahesh. *Transcendental Meditation*. New York: New American Library, 1963.

Zaehner, R.C. *Hindu and Muslim Mysticism*. New York: Schocken Books, 1960.

Glossary

Note: Where a word is used differently in TM and Christianity, meanings (1) and (2) are given.

Absolute (1) In SCI/TM, the ultimate reality of all that is and the Source of all that appears to be to the senses; abstract existence apart from any specific existing thing or person; the supreme deity in philosophical Hinduism, Brahman. (2) In Christianity, the ultimate independent reality and source of all else that exists; God, the distinct, infinite, personal, unchanging and eternal One; the God of Abraham, Isaac, Jacob, Peter, John and Paul.

Absolutes (1) In SCI/TM, there are no absolutes in human knowledge, all knowledge is relative. In the impersonal Absolute there are no principles or assertions. (2) In Christianity, because of the image of God in man, a cognitive revelation and the Bible's inspiration, God's pleasure is revealed in normative principles true for all people everywhere. Examples: Love God with your whole being and your neighbor as yourself.

Abstract (adj.) A quality thought of apart from any particular object or specific thing. Abstract existence is the quality of existence thought of apart from any observable thing that exists.

Agapé In Christianity, a Greek word for a special, self-giving love derived from the Holy Spirit. It refers to God's love for unlovely people in giving His Son for their salvation, also the love of Christians for God and for one another.

Alpha A Greek letter used in certain biofeedback studies for subjective states emphasizing externalized thoughts, remembering, contemplation, power, elation and ease; the brain waves associated with these states.

Atman In TM and Hindu literature, abstract existence (the Absolute) as it manifests itself in a person; the human soul abstracted from the body, the senses, the mind, the intelligence; the innermost, enduring self which changes not and is unqualified by thought and desire; the self that may be identified with Brahman ("I am Brahman").

Atonement In Christianity, the most general term to include all that Jesus Christ accomplished in His death to provide for the restoration of man to divine fellowship and for the removal of all the effects of man's sin. See Also propitiation, reconciliation, redemption.

Being (1) In SCI/TM, the abstract existence underlying all things and persons; that which is in reality, in contrast to illusions, appearances and dreams. There is one kind of being only (monism). (2) In Christianity, the only eternal and ultimate, independent existence is God. After creation there are two kinds of being (a dualism), the eternal Being (God), and dependent temporal being (creation); created being includes angels, demons, man, animals, vegetation and matter-energy. Created beings are not unreal, although they are not the ultimate reality.

Biofeedback A technique for helping a person develop control of internal biological functions (such as heart rate, muscle tension, gastric acid, blood pressure) through his monitoring of electronic instruments measuring them. As this information is fed back to a person, studies show that he can voluntarily control such functions to remarkable degrees.

Guru A Hindu teacher who leads from darkness to light. In SCI/TM used primarily for Guru Dev, the "divine teacher" of Maharishi. "Guru" is not generally used for Maharishi by meditators on the allegation that the method does not depend upon a close relationship of disciple and master.

Brahman A neuter term in Hinduism used for that which is unchanging while the outward forms of things change; the Absolute (1), or ultimate Being (1).

Christianity A religion originating in a linguistic revelation from a personal-infinite God who made the reconciliation of sinners possible through repentance and faith in Jesus as the Christ (Messiah, atoning Saviour) who died for their sins and rose again the third day. Those who trust Christ are regenerated by the Holy Spirit, justified by faith and begin a life of loving adoration, meditation and intercession through the Spirit-illumined Scriptures.

Condemnation In Christianity, a forensic declaration of people's guilt and liability to just punishment as insolent sinners before God's absolute justice.

Consciousness (1) In SCI/TM, assuming that there are not many egos, but only one mind, so there is to be a single state of pure awareness beneath the surface of awareness of ourselves sleeping, dreaming, waking, observing, thinking, etc. TM purports to be the way to this state in which the experiencer is left alone with nothing to experience, a state of pure awareness. (2) In Christianity, each person is created and sustained by God in His image with eternal value and is to be conscious of his identity as a creature, as a sinner, as a believer and as a child of God whose life has dignity, value and meaningful purpose for time and eternity.

Creation The activity of the personal Creator who freely and at a point in the finite past brought the universe into being out of nothing. This view of the world's origin is in contrast with that of emanation.

Creator In Christianity, a personal, eternal Spirit by a fee act of His will brought the world into existence out of nothing including its matter and energy, its people and things. No creature can without blasphemy confuse himself with deity. The Creator-creature dualism is never blured.

Demon A fallen, evil spirit who as an agent of Satanic deception and destruction may afflict people with physical harm, and moral spiritual contamination.

Emanation In contrast to the doctrine of creation, Hinduism explains the origin and structure of reality by an eternal process flowing forth from the divine Being. Since the being of everything issues forth from divine Being, the innermost being of everything is divine.

Expiation In Christianity, a provision of Christ's atonement whereby the sinner's sin is covered, but no reference is made to the turning away of God's wrath as in propitiation.

Faith (1) In SCI/TM, although often used to require no beliefs, TM involves belief in abstract Being as the only reality (monism), one self rather than many selves, the unreality of the observable, changing world of particular things and persons, the efficacy of the TM method and commitment to its practice twice daily. (2) In Christianity, belief in the personal Creator-God, confession of idolatrous worship and service of the creation more than the Creator and of the futility of self-justification, belief that Jesus is the Christ (the divinely given Saviour) who died in our place and rose again from the dead, trust in the living Christ personally for the unmerited gift of His perfect righteousness and eternal life.

Fatherhood of God (1) In SCI/TM, the belief that all people have the same Source, i.e., are particularizations of abstract Being. (2) In Christianity, the belief that all people owe their natural existence to the personal Creator-God (even though morally and spiritually they are not children of God), and the belief that sinners who trust Christ receive the gift of moral and spiritual life and God is their Source both naturally *then spiritually.*

Gospel In Christianity, the good news for people who have offended their Creator, that in His love— *agapé*—for them He gave His eternal Son Jesus Christ to satisfy justice in their behalf by suffering their penalty. Christ's death enabled God to remain just and declare them just. God gave assurance of this to all men by raising Christ from the dead.

Grace In Christianity, the love of God in action bestowing undeserved favor upon us when we are against Him and ourselves and providing for the salvation of all who repent and receive the provisions of redemption.

Hinduism An Indian world-view and way of life based, not on revelation, but nature and mystical experience. The primary writings which convey this ancient religion of India are the *Vedas* and the *Bhagavad-Gita.*

Hypnosis A state resembling deep sleep, but more active in that a person has a little will and feeling of his own, but acts according to the suggestions presented to him; a heightened sense of suggestibility to imagination. In self-hypnotism a person is taught to make suggestions to himself.

International Meditation Society An organization developed by Maharishi Mahesh Yogi to teach SCI/TM to the general public.

Justice A principle of virtue requiring of all men without respect of persons fairness in the treatment of others; giving each exactly what he deserves. This law of decency makes a real difference between good and evil and is not simply the will of the majority, but is binding upon all men of all times everywhere. In Christianity, all are liable to give account to the supreme Administrator of justice, God.

Karma The Hindu term for the law of justice requiring that the accumulated effect of one's actions in this life (assuming transmigration of the soul) determine the type of existence the soul will have in the next life; what you sow you reap.

Kingdom of God In Christianity, the rule of God, His divine kingly authority over: (1) everything that is for temporal purposes, and (2) the people of God by faith who are regenerated or "born" into the rule of redemptive truth and grace. The kingdom of righteousness, peace and joy in the Holy Spirit (Rom. 14:17).

Lila Assuming with Hinduism, that there is but

one divine self, the universe is conceived of as a game (lila) of hide and seek that the divine plays with itself. See also, *maya*.

Maharishi In India a term for a great (maha) saint, sage or teacher (rishi).

Maharishi International University The central educational arm of SCI/TM now located in Fairfield, Iowa.

Mahesh The family name of the founder and leader in SCI/TM, Maharishi Mahesh Yogi.

Mantra A word in Hinduism given by the master to a follower at the time of initiation as a kind of weapon to ward off reasoning, thinking, and conceptualization and unite the meditator with the divine within him. It is a sound without meaning, like OM, the vibrations of which lead to union with one's Source.

Maya Assuming that all experience whatsover is God's, Hinduism believes that all multiplicity, all sensations of limited and separate individuality, of the duality of here and there, I and thou are God's dream (maya). Maya may signify not only illusion but also art and miraculous power.

Meditation (1) In TM, a process of direct experience rather than one of intellectual analysis by which the mind gives attention to refined levels of thinking until going beyond all thought to a state of pure awareness. (2) In Christianity, a discipline of the whole person by which his mind is guided by biblical teaching as his emotions and will are yielded to the illumination of the Holy Spirit to receive the truth of God into his life and interact appropriately with the visible and invisible realities of which that truth speaks.

Monism A view of ultimate reality which asserts

that there are not two or more kinds of real beings, but only one. All real things are one sort of "stuff" or cut out of one piece of goods. Hence a belief that there is no ultimate distinction between matter and spirit, good and evil, or Creator and creature. Hinduism is monistic.

Mysticism (1) A belief that God is totally different than anything the human mind can think and must be approached by a mind without content. In mystical experience a person loses his sense of a personal identity, there are no dualities, time stops and words lose all meaning. Mysticism assumes that divine revelation is non-cognitive, faith does not involve assent to true assertions, religious language is not informative but merely expressive or directive and all words about God are interpreted symbolically. (2) In Christianity, a belief that a personal God who created man's mind in His likeness to think His thoughts after Him, is approached in a personal encounter in which one's identity remains distinct from the Creator-Redeemer, dualities between Creator-creature, good and evil remain, time and history are important in God's plan and biblical promises in human words meaningfully lead to the realities of which they speak. Christian mysticism maintains that divine revelation is cognitive, faith involves belief of true assertions (the gospel) and religious language is informative as well as expressive, and literal with some symbols included.

Nature religion A world-view and way of life, not based on revelation as Judaism, Islam and Christianity, but on observation of life in nature and on transcendence of nature in mystical experience.

Panentheism The doctrine that God includes the world as part of—though not the whole of its Being.

God is believed to be more than the sum total of the parts of the universe in their inner reality. What the "more" is remains undefined, except that it is not personal.

Pantheism The teaching that everything that exists constitutes a unity and that this all-inclusive unity is divine. Pantheism denies the personality of God and equates God with the forces and laws of the universe.

Paradox (1) A logical contradiction for both God and man (non-Christian mysticism), or for man only (Kierkegaard). (2) An apparent logical contradiction for man, but resolvable logically upon further thought. A literary device to attract attention, but not a logical contradiction which affirms and denies the same thing at the same time and in the same respect.

Person A spiritual being who thinks, feels and wills or has self-consciousness and self-determination, or with whom there may be communication and spiritual communion, or morally responsible agent.

Propitiation The provision of Christ's atonement by which His sacrifice of Himself turns away the wrath of God the Father upon the sins of one united to Christ by faith.

Reality In contrast to the illusory, that which actually exists or has being. All that is or exists.

Reconciliation That provision of Christ's atonement by which those united to Christ by faith are no longer estranged from God because of their sin, but restored to loving fellowship with God; an experience of personal encounter guided by the Bible's teaching to the God who is there.

Redemption That provision of Christ's atonement by which believing sinners are liberated progressively from the power of sin—the "slave market" of sin—and are able to say "no!" to temptation.

Regeneration (1) In SCI/TM, a self-transformation through meditation to unfold consciousness of God and achieve self-realization. (2) In Christianity, a radical transformation of the person in which God the Holy Spirit implants the principle of spiritual life renewing the abilities to know, love and serve the Creator rather than creature.

Reincarnation The Hindu belief that the soul moves from one bodily existence to another until after thousands of particular existences, it is released from historical existence and absorbed in the Absolute, Brahman.

Religion A world-view and way of life including: (1) belief in an ultimate power, (2) a sense of human responsibility before the divine power, (3) an awareness of something wrong between man and the divine, (4) a moral code to be obeyed (although often denied), (5) ritual acts to be performed, and (6) a social group of those adopting the world-view and way of life.

Repentance In Christianity, a change of mind, feeling and purpose with respect to all that displeases God (sin). A deliberate determination to cease yielding one's life to the service of concrete or abstract idols and to dedicate one's self to the living God who provided atonement through the cross of Christ, and power to live for Him through the Holy Spirit.

Rishi In Hinduism, a teacher, sage or saint.

Science of Creative Intelligence (SCI) A systematic knowledge (science) about the sources of change in the energy of the universe (evolutionary creativity) leading to a directedness (creativity) in relation to a consciousness of abstract Being, energy and happiness. Another way of expressing the Hindu philosophy of the unreal realm of change in order to experience directly the Source of one's Being, expand his consciousness to the point of lost identity and thus provide bliss.

Source, man's (1) In SCI/TM, man's Source, the goal of all meditation, is believed to be the abstract, impersonal Absolute, or principle of Being and change. (2) In Christianity, the Creator and Lord of the universe who is personal and distinct from all the world's being, however abstract.

Spiritual Regeneration Movement (SRM) An organization designed to teach the SCI/TM philosophy and practice to adults interested in philosophical and ethical values.

Students International Meditation Society (SIMS) An organization founded by the Maharishi Mahesh Yogi for teaching SCI/TM to college and high school students.

Subtle levels of thought In SCI/TM, higher, refined and fine levels of thought. The assumption is that the progression of the mind from attention to more concrete, particular objects to more and more abstract notions until it has no content at all is a superior state of consciousness.

That A term used for the abstract Being which is beyond human language, but is allegedly in all things and persons. The basic teaching of the Hindu *Vedas* and the Maharishi, "I am That, Thou art That, and all this is That."

Transcendental Meditation A form of yoga in which one repeats a mantra to go beyond (transcend) empirical knowledge of particular things in an attempt to become aware of the underlying principle (Source) of all existence.

Transmigration The doctrine that the soul passes at death from one body to another type of bodily existence according to its karma (accumulated merit or demirit). One's soul could reappear as a plant, animal, woman, outcaste (or higher castes) or a god.

Trinity In Christianity, the biblically derived belief that in the unity of the divine essence there are three persons, the Father, the Son, the Holy Spirit, equal in every divine perfection, and executing distinct but harmonious offices in the great work of redemption.

Upanishads Philosophical literature by Indo-Aryans regarding the nature of ultimate truth and reality. This knowledge was regarded sufficient to enable a person to attain emancipation from the causal chain of transmigration and be absorbed in Brahman. The more technically philosophical Vedas.

Vedanta, The A collective term for the philosophy of the Upanishads, the end and goal of the Vedas. The main ideas are: Brahman is reality, the world is illusion and the soul is God.

Vedas The most ancient Hindu books including: (1) a collection of hymns, (2) prose texts on sacrificial rites and ceremonies, (3) advice for the elderly people retired from active life, and (4) the philosophical speculations of the Upanishads. The main ideas are called Vedanta Hinduism.

Yoga In Hinduism, physical and mental discipline to attain a state of well-being through union with the Absolute, Brahman. In the different types of yoga discipline, a person loses his identity and is absorbed in ultimate being.

Yogi A master of one or more methods of yoga who teaches it to others. Maharishi Mahesh Yogi is a teacher of the method of yoga which does not use physical exercises but the repetition of a mantra.